2—

Especially for you
from

TO E.6.
I wish you
great happiness
love
Jul. Hess

The Faux Gourmet

Juli I. Huss

The Faux Gourmet

A Single Woman's Confession
on Food and Sex

A DUTTON BOOK

DUTTON

Published by the Penguin Group
Penguin Books USA Inc., 375 Hudson Street, New York, New York 10014, U.S.A.
Penguin Books Ltd, 27 Wrights Lane, London W8 5TZ, England
Penguin Books Australia Ltd, Ringwood, Victoria, Australia
Penguin Books Canada Ltd, 10 Alcorn Avenue, Toronto, Ontario, Canada M4V 3B2
Penguin Books (N.Z.) Ltd, 182–190 Wairau Road, Auckland 10, New Zealand

Penguin Books Ltd, Registered Offices:
Harmondsworth, Middlesex, England

First published by Dutton, an imprint of Dutton Signet,
a division of Penguin Books USA Inc.
Distributed in Canada by McClelland & Stewart Inc.

First Printing, June, 1994
1 3 5 7 9 10 8 6 4 2

Portions of Chapter One first appeared in Mademoiselle.

REGISTERED TRADEMARK—MARCA REGISTRADA

LIBRARY OF CONGRESS CATALOGING-IN-PUBLICATION DATA
Huss, Juli I.
The faux gourmet : a single woman's confession on food and sex /
Juli I. Huss.
p.   cm.
ISBN 0-525-93806-0
1. Cookery. 2. Cookery—Humor. 3. Sex—Humor.   I. Title.
TX714.H87   1994
641.5—dc20   93-47344
                                                      CIP

Printed in the United States of America
Set in Garamond Light, Bernhard Modern & Bernhard Tango

Designed by Steven N. Stathakis

I dedicate this book to my father, Elmer George Huss, Jr., and my mother, Joan Leahy Huss. I love you both so dearly. With equal love and gratitude I also dedicate this book to Mokichi Okada, who taught me that with patience, my prayers would be answered, and they have been.

Contents

I've been meaning to tell you this for quite some time.
I'm so glad you're here . . .

The Faux Gourmet

Dyeing to Speak to You

I must write very quickly for I am dyeing my hair with L'Oreal's Extra Light Ash Blonde. The fumes are so goddamn strong that I am beginning to have a mystical experience as I form each new bleached-blonde thought. The smell of ammonia mixed with a dash of peroxide is either gonna wind up embalming me from the scalp down or give me one hell of a peach melba blonde swirl. By nature I am a difficult and intense dusky-blonde known for being a better friend than enemy. So, I bleach my hair as a way of working on my personality. I feel it lightens me up.

I am running way behind schedule and am trying to write this opening, dye my hair, plus fold a load of laundry. You see, I am a spermicidally clean person. Not a neat person, but I always have clean cotton washables, and a clean dust ruffle dangling from my bed frame. Unfortunately, my laundry is usually thrown in the middle of my living room floor, forcing me to step over piles of freshly bleached socks and delicate, lacy-thin underpanties, thereby contaminating the fluffy heap with foot dust and other household mung so that I am forced to wash it all over again—repeatedly. A never-ending cycle of fluff and fling.

For this reason alone, it is difficult for me to ever get truly organized. I have a cotton sheet fetish which has also affected the psycho-sexual area of my life profoundly. I have to, absolutely have to, sleep on one-hundred percent solid white cotton sheets that contain absolutely no percale or any synthetic fiber that is manufactured by Monsanto. If I sleep on colored sheets that have a low thread count with loud synthetic botanical prints, I scratch all night long and am prone to extreme dips in my mood by mid-morning the following day. Because—I am trying to scoot this in gracefully and no woman should ever publicly admit this; in fact, I'll deny it to my last dying breath if anyone were to ever confront me in person—I have seen far too many styles and thread counts of synthetic prints in my life as a single woman, and not all were botanical, some were bold checks with narrow pinstripes and a few with a glossy black satin finish.

Guilt. My girlfriend Evie says I suffer from intense guilt for having made such a mess out of my life. Which is really an odd reaction coming from a woman who could only eat food that came in "to go" cups and containers. For years, Evie only felt comfortable with hand-delivered food whose packaging could be tossed away upon ingestion. She positively could not make the commitment to feed herself. Also being single, taking the time to actually cook food for her own well-being seemed, in her opinion, "a boring waste of time." So instead, Evie ate standing up, ready to disembark from her life at a moment's notice. Her behavior with food reflected her behavior with men. She had a "to go" style of relationships with men that appeared piping hot and ready, but often left her standing alone feeling cold to the touch, and eventually just emotionally emptied—tossed away. She, too, was rather high spirited in the psycho-sexual arena and would only confess this if plied with a couple of good stiff vodka stingers, no ice. Frankly, I was a little appalled when she remarked that I had made a mess out of my life since it was her life I was patterning mine after.

Evie is the reason I wrote this book. If it weren't for those sticky, hot nights sitting out on her twenty-fourth-floor terrace overlooking the herds of sweating vacationers strolling through Central Park, I doubt this thing would have ever been written. Her terrace became the place where we'd confess our failures to each other, the lost loves, the failed diets, the bounced checks. Evie would take a hit off her vodka stinger and I'd take a hit off my bag of Cheetos and the conversation would spill out into the black hazy night. Sometimes if Evie had taken one too many hits off her stinger, she'd lean over the balcony and stare out into the shadowy greens of the park. It was a spectacular view, acres of lush forest greens that were speckled with all sorts of flickering dots of colored lights. Often she'd trail off talking about her longing for someone to love, heave a long heavy sigh, then turn and ask me to pass her a Cheeto. It seemed that food was a gentle comfort to her loneliness. Some nights we'd be more inspired than others. We'd make lists of what we ate when we were angry, when we were lonely and when we felt lost. Food was the one thing that would love us in a way that we could not love ourselves.

Evie always called me when there was a thunderstorm warning. No matter what time, she'd call and I would run over. We'd sit out in the hot, pressing haze with our feet propped up on the red clay brick and wait for the eruption to begin. There was nothing more soothing to us than the violent crack of lightning from a summer thunderstorm. When the rain would begin to fall it would release a pressure lock of sadness within us, a hopeless sadness from the incredible lack of intimacy in our lives and of not knowing how to change in a way that would make love not feel so isolating and painful. The loud clap of thunder would be very calming to us and would relieve that twisting pressure—for a moment. But no matter what the weather forecast, our conversations always centered around food, love and the eternal search for some dignity. The last time we did this was well over a year ago. It was a long, lonely, muggy summer, but one that lifted a lot of illusions about who we were as single women. I always say that last summer was the one that taught me how to hope.

Hang out a minute. . . . I have to check my roots and make sure I'm not gonna wind up looking like Carol Channing.

Tonight is a very momentous occasion for me because I am celebrating the completion of this book with the three girlfriends who allowed me to share with you their search for hope and dignity in their lives as single women. The plans were originally to have a beautiful, gourmet dinner with pink linens and fresh flowers over at my place. But—and I say this as a way of letting you know that I am not an overachiever—those plans have been dashed because I do not have the time or psychic energy to crank out a lavish, full-flowered, linen luau. I am botanically tapped out. You see, I have become a very clever cook over this past year and have learned two very important culinary lessons:

1. Don't date creeps or perverts.
2. Reawaken your appreciation for potluck.

At seven o'clock the four gals are meeting near the petting zoo in Central Park for a light spring picnic. Evie called earlier today and said she would get there a little early and lay out the blanket and light up the candelabra. My girlfriend Sharon, who's flown in from Dallas for the occasion, is bringing some dessert thing with bananas. (Relations between Sharon and me are still a little strained, so when she called this morning, I didn't press the issue. She's a little touchy about me—don't want to spring that vicious trap of hers.) And my wonderful friend Karen is bringing a special broccoli dish she created all on her own. I, Junie Bell Lake, am responsible for the main course, which is going to be fried chicken. Which I am reheating at this very moment. It's embarrassing to admit this, but . . . I didn't have time to actually fry it up myself, so I went to the cleverest cook in town, Colonel Sanders—Mr. Kentucky Fried. It's a little tacky, but I figure if I stick the drumsticks and thighs and chubby breasts into a cute wicker basket with a checkered napkin, no one is going to press me on the chicken's actual incarnation. I did make a fabulous ginger-peanut cole slaw that is so refreshing and packed with so much zing that I am sure it will help add to the overall homemade effect. It's a truly inspired cole slaw made with white cabbage, fresh ginger, Granny Smith apple and a pinch of red onion, topped with a handful of crushed peanuts. It is soooo good. And the dressing is just a couple of lemons squeezed up with some soy sauce and sesame oil.

Hang on a minute. . . . I have to call Evie and make sure she's handling the drinks. Sharon will have a fit if we forget to bring Dr. Pepper.

———

The only person I am sorry won't be coming tonight is Carolyn Snorkel, Sharon's mother, who is, to this day, my personal heroine. The woman is a fucking saint. I spoke to her earlier today about this book for over an hour on the telephone from my fluffy white bed. She decided to stay in Dallas and wash her array of flaming auburn wigs instead of make the trip. She's such a dear woman. I had sent her the manuscript a week ago and she called to let me know it was a bit crude and revealing in places, but overall she liked it. Her opinion means more to me than anyone. As she spoke, little tiny tears slid down my cheeks as I realized that today I no longer have that twister of sadness swelling inside of me. I laid it to rest the day I learned how to feed myself. Mrs. Snorkel said something to me that keeps running over and over in my thoughts. "When a woman can feed herself full of the right things, she is free to love the world around her."

Today, I know that freedom she spoke about and I hope that in your life, you will too.

Now, I've got to go rinse this stuff off my hair 'cause it is starting to get me all misty-eyed.

Your comrade in the kitchen,
Junie Bell Lake
THE ONLY FAUX GOURMET
May 17, 1993
New York City
4:35 p.m.

Part I

The Clever Cook's Rude Awakening

The Rise and Fall and Rebirth of a Clever Cook

Sharon Snorkel Lovit was born a clever cook. Which is a remarkable quality when you stop and consider that Sharon has the emotional depth of an acrylic birdbath.

You see, Sharon is one of those people who stays with you throughout your entire life like a venereal disease. We met back in 1979 in Atherton, California, at Menlo College during the roommate selection lottery. We both lost and wound up rooming with each other during our freshman year. Sharon was originally from Plano, Texas, and my first impression of her was that she was the type of girl Elvis probably would have slept with during his final days. She was sort of a cross between Cleopatra and Miss Ellie—kind of slutty, yet kind of not. Sharon was difficult to define since most of her role models came from *The Young and the Restless*—there wasn't a lot of content but she had vast amounts of raw data on topics like water retention, yeast infections, oral sex tips, diamond-studded press-on fingernails and how to keep breasts afloat in a strapless dress.

I have witnessed every major turning point in her life. I was there moments after she lost her virginity—for the third time. ("Always let him think he's the first, baby. Even if you did Roger his uncle at the Army-Navy game last fall. That's all ancient history today, sugar.") I was there to hold her hand when the news broke that Victoria Principal would not be returning to "Dallas" the following season, which was the first televised death of a role model for Sharon. ("She was the only *true* star on that show, honey. Why, Pamela Ewing could mop the floor with Sue Ellen and could kick that mean ol' J.R. right in the onions with just a look. . . . Katharine Hepburn would give her eye teeth to have her talent, and you can quote me on that.")

Whenever Sharon was depressed, she would crawl up onto her pink satin bedspread, pull her black luscious curls into a mile-high hairdo and say, "Pass me the Final Net, will you honey? I'm havin' a frightful lookin' hair night. I've got to stay in tonight and see if Sue Ellen is ever gonna git sober. She's such a mess these days, sleepin' around with cowhands now. Doesn't she realize she has a reputation to uphold in the Dallas–Fort Worth community? Oh, and if any men—and I am being very generous using that word—call for me this evening, you tell them I am at the Cannes Film Festival this weekend."

Passing her the Final Net, I said, "Sharon, you are going to get busted if you say you are at the Cannes Film Festival. It's not until the summer."

"Well, who in the hell are you, Nostradramus? You don't have to tell them that. Besides, men love it when you blow a little blue smoke up their asses. Makes 'em hunger for your glamour. Which, by the way, you could stand a little more of, honey. Here, take this can of Final Net and pile your fuzz up into something real big and fluffy. Go ahead and spray your brains out."

On nights like these while Sharon was warming up her Sony Trinitron portable color television, she would fix her favorite culinary fare: Gerber Baby Food mashed bananas cupped in dollops of Cool Whip nondairy whipped topping, scooped up with Nabisco vanilla wafers and all washed down with a frosty glass of Dr. Pepper with plenty of crushed ice. "If I were back in Plano, I would put a sprig of fresh mint in the glass to refresh the bubbles. It's times like this that I get terribly homesick for the refinements of Southern livin'," she said, sighing during a Summer's Eve commercial.

I never knew fresh mint leaves could actually refresh carbonated prune juice, but in honor of my long-standing friendship with Sharon, let this be considered your first cooking tip.

About twice a year we get together to celebrate some ground-breaking event in each others' lives. I'm sure I would be right in saying that mine is always the last invitation to be sent out. Like when she got married in 1983 to Mr. Sammy Lovit from "the ol' San Antonio road, gal," as he would always say while winking at me.

Now, Sammy was a scum bag and he made no bones about it. I actually liked Sammy for the fact that he never pretended to be anything more than the rattlesnakin', money-suckin', panty-chasin' slab of brainless beef that he was. Sammy was sort of a cross between the Reverend Jim Jones and Jack LaLane. He always wore those shiny nylon jogging suits that look so ridiculous on men, with iguana testicle-skin boots and a cowboy hat with a feather from some kind of dead bird. A genuine piece of work, that Sammy Lovit.

"Now you git on over here and give the Lovin' Man a big hug, gal, 'cause the Sammin' Man loves a big blonde and you are it," he said as he snapped my bra strap in the TWA terminal at the Dallas–Ft. Worth Airport.

"You ever touch me like that again, Sammy, and your dick will be dangling from my key chain. Do you read me, Bubba?" I whispered in a hot breath that fogged up his metalicized Ray Ban's.

At the time Sharon and I hadn't seen each other in well over a year. I had transferred to UC Berkeley and she had gone on a two-year job search for something that would still enable her to wear her three-inch press-on nails. "I told you the Sam Man would love you now didn't I, Junie Lake?" was what this rather overdressed woman with Morgan Fairchild blonde hair said to me as she snuggled up between me and her man.

"Oh Christ . . . Sharon, is that you? You look like somebody off the set of 'Dynasty.' "

"I know it. People tell me that all day long. They say I have shades of Linda Evans in me and I'm just tickled shitless. Now I got you a Coca Cola and told 'em to put it in a commuter cup so you wouldn't drool on the ride home. 'Cause baby girl, you're goin' to a Texas barbecue tonight and I want you lookin' good."

To be quite frank, I can't remember the difference between the pre-wedding barbecue, the wedding-day barbecue brunch and the wedding barbecue dinner. Don't ask me why, but the whole time I was there I thought I was at Barbara Cartland's coronation. Everybody just sort of looked like her—even the men. There were lots of ferns, ladies in lavender ostrich-feather beaded evening gowns and pink carnations, and huge silver bowls of barbecue sauce. "That's Texan holy water out here, gal!" chirped Sammy from behind his stud-man sunglasses.

You'll have to forgive me, but I was suffering from panic attacks at the time and had taken a small handful of Xanex to get a grip on the weekend. I was teetering on the verge of a walking coma and kept knocking over bowls of barbecue sauce in desperate search of the Porto-toilets. Sharon told me a few years later when we were celebrating her divorce from Sam the Lovin' Man that I was a "liquor-tongued assholian blob. You are no longer invited to a celebration of mine as long as I live in the state of Texas, Junie Lake. Why, I came downstairs the morning of my wedding and asked if I could make you a Texas-sized pig 'n a blanket for breakfast and you told me not to bother waking him up until the priest arrived. Do you know how much that hurt me? Why, I should have just cut you out of my life back then."

Now, I can tell from the wedding pictures that, as usual, Sharon had done a beautiful job organizing her special day of union with Sammy Lovit. The only problem I had was with her ice sculpture of a desert cactus, which during the celebration had melted down into the shape of some kind of wild coyote phallus. (A very strange centerpiece that everyone found a bit unnerving. Happy guests would stare at it, then shudder and pretend they didn't see what they thought they saw and reach for a caraway seed dinner roll.) It was a bit too primal an edifice to spring on a group like that. But her food selection looked beautiful in the wedding book. In order to make Sharon happy, I am duty bound to include the recipes from her wedding menu: roasted Cornish game hens in an orange sauce with golden raisin–wild rice stuffing, honey-glazed carrots and a citrus garden salad with a tangy vinaigrette dressing. This is the same salad dressing that Sharon has made over the years, and let it be known that there is no known over-the-counter drug on the market that will unblock your sinuses quite the way her "tangy" fruit-filled vinaigrette will. Oh yeah, I almost forgot. Sharon also made a Virgin's Day Banana Cream Cake that was pretty tasty but a bit mushy for me. Honestly, I thought her menu was passable for food that went out of style during the sixties. (You know, it's very difficult to talk behind someone's back in a book.)

I refuse, absolutely refuse to give you the recipe for her roasted Cornish game hen in orange sauce. Trust me, they may have looked beautiful, but they were awful. If the truth must be known, Cornish game hens are so tiny and bony and such a pain in the ass to deal with that I can't in good conscience encourage any clever cook to get involved with them. You can never have a good relationship with these birds because of the constant tug-of-war between too many bones and too little meat. All of the guests at the wedding were hand wrestling their slippery hens off the edge of their plates. The only one I saw handle the bird with any real flair was Mrs. Snorkel's toy poodle Eclair, who wrestled the wild game to the ground and flung the skinny carcass against the leg of a picnic bench. Alas, exhausted from her Kung Fu death grip, Eclair sought refuge in an abandoned peppermint Tic Tac left on the ground. Listen, when the family dog won't even reap her conquered rewards, a clever cook must see it as a sign. But if there are any readers who insist upon having this recipe, you can call Sharon in Plano, Texas. Better yet, call her *collect*.

As for her recipe for golden raisin–wild rice stuffing . . . okay, I'll include that one. It's very good when served with a simple roasted tarragon chicken which was the original fowl I had suggested she use for her wedding dinner. Sharon makes a terrific roasted tarragon chicken that has a mouth-watering, sweet succulence in every bite. Because of her great cooking instinct, Sharon's chicken always has a special taste and aroma. Like myself, she rarely follows a recipe. Instead, she figures out what she thinks would be best for her bird. Sharon stuffs the carcass with tiny boiling onions, chopped celery and fresh tarragon leaves to insure a moist, rich flavor. Then she tents the bird with aluminum foil and roasts it until the juices run clear and glossy when pricked with a fork. (If the juices from a chicken have a pinkish, milky cast, then it is not fully cooked.) It's a crime she did not go with this bird.

Absolutely *no*, a big Nancy Reagan *no*, on her honey-glazed carrots—they were gross. I am replacing them with a terrific recipe she uses for creamed horseradish carrots that are so fabulous, so easy to make and have a wonderful, creamy yet zesty bite to them. Again, this was a recipe Sharon created all by herself. She thought the hot tang of horseradish coupled with the mellowing effect of half 'n' half would add an interesting flavor to the sweetness of carrots. It amazes me how a girl so shallow can be this clever. A mind boggler, isn't she?

In regard to her tangy vinaigrette, I'm going to have to veto that too. Her secret to that dressing is adding enough red-wine vinegar to make your eyes tear—she thinks it lowers the caloric intake. Like most clever cooks, she really screws the pooch every once in a while, but this never throws her confidence in the kitchen. "Well, if you don't like it, then you make your own damn dressing," is how she responded to my critique. She's difficult but clever.

Am I going to include her Virgin's Day Banana Cream Cake recipe, you ask? Yes, I will, but I am not going to showcase it in my opening chapter.

Sharon and Mrs. Snorkel oversaw the catering of the wedding dinner. All of the recipes were developed from Sharon's vivid imagination. Because she's a sentimental sort, Sharon wanted to make all of the food herself to give her wedding a personal feel. A catering staff was hired, but Sharon, Mama Snorkel and I spent most of our time doing all the prep work on her wedding extravaganza. Sharon was a true Nazi in the kitchen, which forced me to rely on a larger dose of bite-size relaxants and alcoholic solvents than were probably necessary. People rarely ever think of Sharon as a bitch in the classic sense because most people confuse sweetness with sincerity. By appearances Sharon is always just lilac-colored frou-frou with a ton of hairspray and a lacy southern drawl. What roams behind all that manipulative innocence is a hammerhead shark neatly zipped up into a sardine suit. God help you if you happen to get in her way.

Of course we got into a fight. That goes without saying.

As I eyeballed three cardboard boxes of naked birds, I hollered, "You want me to disembowel two hundred and fifty Cornish game hens and then stuff them? That's what I've flown down here to do?"

"Just hush up and do it," she said as she slapped a featherless scoundrel into my hands.

She was using me. Sharon would never ask one of her snotty, debutante bridesmaids to do this type of shit work. "They all have maids, Junie. They don't do work like this." If it wasn't for Mama Snorkel, I would have walked out of the kitchen right then and there. This is the nature of my relationship with Sharon. I could never be in her bridal party, but I could dig the guts out of her goddamn bony birds. But our friendship was always like this. Like the morning after she banged Billy Guenther and was convinced she had syphilis. It wasn't Bunny Foobar she dragged to the gynecologist, it was me. And I let her use my name on the patient information sheet. She had cystitis, but I sat in the doctor's office and read off the symptoms of a syphilis sufferer from the pamphlet on the wall while we waited for the doctor to see her. Look, I guess it's a two-way street. A few months later as I lay screaming into my pillow, Sharon was the one who poured my urine spec into the test tube and waited to see if my dot turned pink or white. Now, how many

friends will take your pregnancy test for you? It is solely
for the reason that Sharon is the only friend I know who
would handle my urine that I gutted her lousy birds. But
we fought anyway.

"Sammy is a fornicating moron," I said, jamming my
fist into the bird's cavity.

"How dare you speak about Sammy Lovit like that.
Get out of my kitchen."

I hissed as I flung another stuffed carcass onto the
pile. "I betcha ten bucks he's gonna try to poke one of
your bridesmaids before the day is over."

"And you wonder why I didn't ask you to be my
maid of honor," she said, slamming the oven door.

I said shitty things about her to every guest I met at
the wedding. I think something must have gotten back
to her because our conversations were rather cool for a
long time afterward. (Well, I think a lot of things got back
to her about what I did at her wedding, but I'll get to that
later.) Sharon's marriage was absolute bliss until she
found out that Sammy was banging an Herbalife trainee
three weeks after the wedding ceremony. Which was really amazing when you consider that they spent two
weeks honeymooning in Barbados. For a long time
Sharon pretended not to listen to what her instincts were
telling her. She knew Sammy was screwing everything in
sight, but she pretended that everything was "*Fab-u-
lous.*" Sometimes on the telephone she'd say something
cryptic like, "He's got his hands full right now. I'm just
not sure with what." Most of the time when she phoned
it was about cooking. "Can you send me a case of oyster
sauce from Chinatown? I can't find any here." In the early
days of the marriage Sharon was into Chinese cooking,
but as time wore on she lost trust in her intuition and
stopped cooking altogether. "It's just cold and hard by
the time he gets home. I usually just heat him up something in the microwave." By the time she found the pair

of torn pantyhose stuffed in the pocket of his lime-green jogging suit, she had to lie to herself about what she knew, and the cleverness of her cooking vanished. Sammy humiliated Sharon with his relentless philandering, and in turn, Sharon took it out on herself. She went through the hairstyles of the entire cast of "Dynasty" and then moved on to "Knots Landing." She started to get paranoid that Sammy was screwing all of her girlfriends. "Did you ever . . . ?" she whispered late one night into the phone. "Never," I said before she could finish the sentence.

Soon she stopped returning friends' calls on her answering machine. She trusted no one, not even herself. Her days were spent frantically getting the house and herself ready for his arrivals. By the time he'd get home, she'd feed him dinner, they'd have three minutes of sex and he'd fall asleep watching television on the living room couch. Sharon didn't sleep much at night and would walk around paranoid and exhausted during the day. It seemed like every few months when things started to become nice and stable between the two of them, Sammy would betray her and come home with the scent of another woman.

Sharon always had a fabulous figure. Ample breasts with a tiny waist and cute little cheerleader legs. During her marriage she starved herself into a sexual skeleton to hold back the betrayal she felt so deeply in her spirit. She couldn't eat because it brought up too many feelings— too much rage. If she let her rage come out she was afraid she might kill herself. (Well, she certainly thought about it a lot.) Sharon's depression dulled her usual protective cunning by making her feel sleepy and bloated. When she wasn't consumed with paranoid fantasies, she was possessed with anxiety about what she looked like. The case of oyster sauce I had sent her went unopened. She became too preoccupied with looking prettier than all the women she saw on television. Her age was another drag on her psyche, feeling old and worn out at twenty-eight. "I just feel so haggard all the time, I think I need to rest. But Sammy and I are really good. He's real busy, running around town. . . . It's just me, Junie. Something's not right with me." The more she lied to herself the thinner she got. By the time Sharon confronted Sammy about the found pantyhose, he felt it was best to let her think his running around was her fault. "You just don't turn me on the way you used to. You used to be so much fun and now you're like my mother, all crazy and depressed. I need a woman who knows how to be free and easy with her body," Sammy said to her during an argument over why Sharon never got out of her bathrobe. She lied to herself again when she believed him.

The fall of a clever cook.

The best thing she ever did for herself was to dump that fornicating son-of-a-bitch. She got her life back. Although it didn't feel that way for a couple of years after the divorce. For almost two years straight, Sharon drove around Dallas in her yellow four-door Seville screaming until her throat was dry and raw. Yep, that's right, she screamed her way back into some semblance of sanity. The betrayal she felt so deeply inside herself was eating her up and the only way she was going to get better was by pushing that anger up and out of her. Instead of turning that anger on herself, though, she found a way to get rid of it. Hearing the sound of her own voice made her finally listen to what was buried within her spirit. She finally heard herself think. "I put my tortured tears into the wind, Junie. I just opened my lungs and started screaming, and two years later I stopped." She found that all of the years she had spent analyzing what was wrong with her had kept her from leaving that permanently erected, rat-faced bastard. "I remember lying around the house day after day wondering what it was that *I* was doing wrong. I begged him to go into therapy, I begged him to talk with our minister, I begged him to tell me what was wrong with me. But nothing changed him."

When Sharon started screaming she woke herself up. (And probably anybody else within the city limits, sleeping or dead.) After the screaming came the crying. "I'd scream all the way to a stop light and then I'd cry. As soon as the light turned green, I'd start screaming again and hit the gas." She screamed and cried so much that her insomnia turned into sheer physical exhaustion, and she was finally able to get some sleep. Sleep was like an answered prayer for Sharon.

Up until she was able to sleep, Sharon had been living on Vick's cough drops, Swiss Miss Instant Hot Chocolate and Beer Nuts. "The day I started to feed myself was the day I accepted that I was never going back to him. When I ate, I knew it was over." The first meal she made for herself was Granny Snorkel's meat loaf with mashed potatoes and lima beans. "I remember waking up on a rainy Saturday afternoon craving Granny's meat loaf. I drove to the store and got all of the ingredients. It felt so strange to be cooking for myself. I felt so vulnerable, like I'd be embarrassed if someone walked in and caught me feeding just myself. I made this little baby meat loaf and stuck it in the oven while I boiled a couple of peeled potatoes. My house was dark and quiet, so I lit some candles and put on my favorite Barry Manilow tape. I remember singing as I mashed the potatoes. I hadn't sung since Sammy told me I had a lousy voice. It felt so good to sing along with Barry. I set a place at the dining room table using all of my wedding china. I think I'd used it twice while we were married. It felt so good just to sit at a beautiful table and eat warm food. There was something so safe and kind about it. I think it was the first meal I had really let myself enjoy since I had gotten married."

Sharon made it a nightly ritual to come home after an evening of wheeling around Dallas–Fort Worth screaming her head off and fix herself a hot meal. Her life got better, but in all honesty it took a good couple of years before she could really begin to trust herself. The constant betrayal had really damaged Sharon's instinct to nurture, and she needed plenty of time to get her dignity back, but she slowly began to rebuild her hope and faith. Cooking helped her to see that she could take care of herself, and she grew to have faith in herself through all the difficult decisions that awaited her in her new life. Learning how to feed herself again allowed her to set a new foundation as a single woman, a foundation that couldn't be taken away by anyone. You know, you can give your soul away, but nobody can ever take it from you.

For her thirty-first birthday present to herself, Sharon flew to Waikiki to attend an Anthony Robbins seminar. It seems that Barry Manilow and Anthony Robbins were Sharon's spiritual saviors during this whole ordeal. On her way back, she decided to drop by New York City to visit me. Well, that's sort of true. It seems that she met a lovely man while at the seminar. "He's forty-two, a political consultant—a Republican, thank you, Jesus—circumcised, divorced with two kids, in daily contact with his inner child, and lives right here in New York—but I really did want to see you too, Junie. I'm just up here to check out his base of operations before I start handing over any body parts," she said, unpacking her Neiman Marcus makeup kit. These days Sharon looks like a cross between Marie and Donny Osmond.

(And let me tell you, Sharon could have gone the rest of her life without ever seeing me. Don't think for one minute that I don't know she is using me.)

It had been about three years since Sharon had been with anybody. "Sex is earned, honey. The only place you find immediate unconditional love is in heaven. My love is very conditional these days and so is my affection," Sharon yelled from my bathroom as she shimmied into her pink demi-cup, push-up padded bra. (I know, I am also wondering how she knows he's circumcised.)

"He just has that look of a guy who is circumcised." She's bull-shitting all of us now, but what am I going to do? If she wants to play Virgin Miss USA again, then I guess I can witness her deflowering for a fourth time . . . or is it her fifth? God, there have been so many with her that it makes me dizzy. (And it kills me because I was always the one saddled with the reputation for being an easy lay. I may have to try the virgin routine myself.)

Do you want to know what Sharon's boyfriend's name is? Roland Farmdale. Doesn't that name just make you want to lie down and puke all over yourself?

Anyway, since I have her here with me, I think I am going to totally ixnay all of her wedding recipes. They were all *shit*. I was just trying to be nice, but I can see that it's not going to work. So just forget everything I said. What I am going to do instead is have Sharon sit down and write out all of the recipes she used when she entered the "Scream-and-Sauté" period of her separation. I think these recipes would be much more inspiring for burgeoning clever cooks.

"It just kills me that you are not going to use my wedding dinner to start your book. And I was going to provide illustrated color pictures and everything. . . ."

Oh, will somebody tell her to just fuck off?

MS. SHARON SNORKEL LOVIT

Dear Sweet, Lovely Readers,

I am Junie's oldest and dearest friend and I am happy to meet you all. Since the day I met Junie she is the most screwed up person I have ever met. But what can I say; she is like a sister to me. And I know she has said some terrible things about me because she won't let me read the first half of this chapter.

Now I am going to give Junie some of my best recipes for learning how to feed yourself during a divorce or a major breakup. It's a rocky road out there, gals, and you've got to prepare yourself to really let it all hang out. Please don't worry if you don't make them perfectly. Junie and I both agree that the most important thing is that you feed yourself. Don't worry about anything else. Because, gals, let me tell you, if I can get through it, so can you!

DON'T FORGET TO SCREAM!!!

> *Lots of hugs and kisses.*
> *Sharon Snorkel Lovit*

PS. If you are ever in Dallas, call me, and I'll fix us lunch . . .

Oh Jesus, here we go, she's taken over my book.

Nonetheless, she has made up some practical, inexpensive recipes that will come in handy if you are going through a difficult time in life. In situations like Sharon's, the screaming phase is just as important as the sauté phase. If you don't go through the cycle of screaming and crying, the rage just stays locked within your psyche. Women need to hear the magnitude of their disappointment or else they take it out on themselves by either stuffing or starving. In either case it's a betrayal—an act of anger turned inward. So put this book down and go scream your guts out . . . and when you've gained some composure, try one of Sharon's recipes and feed yourself. You'll feel better.

Now I have to go find her a pair of control-top pantyhose for her date with Roland Dripface Farmdale.

Granny Snorkel's Hometown Meat Loaf

SERVES 4 TO 6

2 pounds lean ground
   chuck (hamburger)
1 egg
2 cloves garlic, minced
1 cup diced yellow onions
½ cup diced sweet red
   pepper
2 tablespoons chopped
   fresh parsley

4 tablespoons chopped
   fresh celery leaves
4 tablespoons soy sauce
4 tablespoons red wine
¾ cup bread crumbs
4 tablespoons ketchup
Salt and pepper to taste
3 strips raw bacon (see
   Note)

Preheat oven to 350 degrees. In a large mixing bowl, combine all the ingredients together using your hands. (Remove rings and other delicate family heirlooms from hands and wrists before plunging into mixture!)

Shape the meat mixture into the size of a small loaf of bread and spread, using fingers of course, a thin layer of ketchup over the top. Set the loaf in an 8 × 10-inch foil-lined baking pan. Place the strips of bacon on top of meat loaf and bake uncovered for 1 hour.

Note: I think the reason Granny Snorkel wasn't around to fix this for Sharon was that she ate too much bacon. If you are health conscious, forego the bacon and sprinkle 2 tablespoons of bread crumbs on top instead.

Sinfully Creamy Mashed Potatoes

SERVES 2

*2 large Idaho or Russet
   potatoes*
¼ cup milk

2 tablespoons butter
2 ounces cream cheese
Salt and pepper to taste

Scrub and peel the potatoes. (Some people like their mashed potatoes with the skins on; c'est a vous—use your own judgment.) Cut them into large cubes and place them in a saucepan with 1 quart of salted water. Boil for 20 minutes, or until tender when pricked with a fork. Remove from the stove and drain the water.

Add the milk, butter, cream cheese, salt and pepper and mash with a potato ricer, sturdy fork or hand mixer on low speed. (Be careful not to overbeat if using a hand mixer; great mashed potatoes are always lumpy.)

If you think your potatoes are a little dry, add 2 tablespoons of milk.

Roasted Bell Pepper Pasta

SERVES 2 TO 3

1 medium green bell
    pepper
1 medium red bell pepper
1 medium yellow bell
    pepper
⅓ cup olive oil
1 medium red onion,
    thinly sliced
½ cup pitted black olives,
    halved lengthwise
2 large cloves garlic,
    minced

6 anchovy fillets
½ pound thin spaghetti
1 cup feta cheese,
    crumbled
2 tablespoons chopped
    basil
2 tablespoons chopped
    parsley
Salt and pepper to taste

To roast the peppers: Line the broiler pan with foil, place the peppers on it and set the pan as close as possible to the flame. (A countertop toaster oven also works well.) Broil until the peppers are charred on the outside. You want them blacker than black to pick up the smoky flavor. Remove the blackened peppers from broiler and allow them to cool to room temperature. Slice them in half, remove the core and seeds and carefully peel off the blackened skins. Cut the peppers into paper-thin strips and set aside, saving as much of their own juice as humanly possible. (Roasting peppers is indeed a bitch, but you can save time by roasting a bunch of them at once and packing them in an air-tight container in olive oil and storing in the refrigerator. They should keep for at least a month if stored properly.)

    Pour the olive oil into a skillet and over a medium-low heat sauté the onions, garlic and olives until tender. Add the anchovies and roasted peppers. Set aside and keep warm.

Put three quarts of water in a large pot along with 1 tablespoon of salt and 2 tablespoons of olive oil. Cook the pasta according to package directions and drain.

Transfer the pasta to a serving dish and toss with the roasted pepper mixture. Add the feta cheese, basil and parsley and toss until well blended. Serve warm or cold.

Curried Tofu and Brown Rice Casserole

SERVES 2 TO 4

2 tablespoons butter
1 medium onion, chopped
1 clove garlic, chopped
1 bay leaf
1 cup uncooked brown
    rice
1 tablespoon curry powder
1 teaspoon ground
    cinnamon
2½ cups chicken broth
2 stalks celery, chopped

1 carrot, chopped
1 firm cake of tofu, cut
    into cubes and
    soaked in ¼ cup of
    soy sauce
½ cup raisins
1 Granny Smith apple,
    cored and cut into
    bite-size pieces
½ cup toasted almonds
    for garnish

In a large skillet, melt the butter and add the onion, garlic and bay leaf. Sauté until onions are translucent. Add the rice, curry powder and cinnamon and continue to sauté. Add the chicken broth and bring to a boil, stirring constantly. Add the celery and carrot and cover. Reduce the heat to low and cook for 45 minutes to an hour, or until rice is tender.

Drain the tofu and add to the skillet along with the raisins and apple. If the dish seems a little dry, add ¼ cup more chicken stock and cook for another 10 minutes. Garnish with toasted almonds.

Note: This recipe may be cooked in a large covered casserole dish in a 350-degree preheated oven if you prefer. Prepare the recipe through the cooking of the rice as stated in stove-top recipe, cover the casserole and check after 45 minutes for tenderness of rice. When the rice is tender, add the drained tofu, raisins and apple and cook for 10 more minutes. Garnish with toasted almonds.

Sharon's Camembert Soufflé

SERVES 2 TO 3

2 tablespoons butter
3 tablespoons flour
1 cup milk
1 cup camembert cheese,
    cubed, rind and all
4 egg yolks
½ cup finely chopped
    scallions
1 teaspoon salt

½ teaspoon cayenne
    pepper
6 egg whites
1 teaspoon cream of
    tartar
¼ cup grated Parmesan
    cheese
1 tablespoon chopped
    fresh parsley

Preheat the oven to 350 degrees. In a large saucepan over a low heat, melt the butter and add the flour gradually until it makes a thick paste-like texture. (Soufflés are really easy. Don't get freaked out.)

Slowly whisk in the milk and continue stirring until a smooth, thick batter forms, about 5 minutes. Add the camembert and continue cooking until all of the cheese melts. Remove the batter from the heat and allow to cool for 10 minutes. Beat in egg yolks, scallions, salt, cayenne pepper, and chopped parsley. Set the pan aside.

In a large mixing bowl beat the egg whites with the cream of tartar using a hand mixer until stiff white peaks form. Slowly pour the cheese mixture into the egg whites and thoroughly blend. Set the batter aside.

Butter and flour a 2-quart soufflé dish (or any oven-proof dish that measures 8 inches across and 3 inches in depth). Cover the bottom of the soufflé dish with the Parmesan cheese and slowly pour the soufflé batter into the dish. Bake for 35 to 40 minutes, or until the soufflé begins to pull from the sides of the dish and it has a spongy texture. Serve immediately.

Note: If you want to make a small soufflé for a single serving, use a 4-inch ceramic ramekin and cut the recipe in half. Bake for about 15 minutes.

Camembert soufflé with a spinach salad and crusty bread make a delicious meal.

Fruit-for-Life Salad with Lime Dressing and Warmed Granola Crunch Topping

SERVES 2

¼ cup raspberries
¼ cup blueberries
½ cup strawberries, stemmed and thinly sliced
½ cucumber, peeled, seeded and thinly sliced
1 medium orange, peeled and sliced into bite-size pieces
½ cup seedless green grapes
1 tablespoon chopped fresh mint
1 tablespoon orange juice
Lime Dressing (recipe follows)
Warmed Granola Crunch Topping (recipe follows)

Wash all the berries carefully so as not to crush them and gently pat them dry on a paper towel. Peel and seed the cucumber and wash and stem the grapes. Put all the fruit and cucumber in a large bowl, add the freshly chopped mint and orange juice and gently toss. Store in refrigerator until ready to serve.

When ready to serve, drizzle dressing over salad, and sprinkle topping over all. Serve immediately.

Lime Dressing

½ cup nonfat yogurt
1 teaspoon lime zest
1 tablespoon lemon juice
1 tablespoon honey

Combine all the ingredients and pour on salad just before serving.

Warmed Granola Crunch Topping

1 cup granola   *½ cup honey*

Preheat oven to 350 degrees.

In a small mixing bowl combine the granola and honey. Sprinkle mixture on an ungreased cookie sheet and bake for 8 to 10 minutes.

Allow to cool a bit and sprinkle warmed topping over fruit salad.

From the Kitchen of Junie Lake

Five Tips from a Clever Cook

Tip #1: Remove wine stains from a cotton or linen tablecloth by rubbing a teaspoon of table salt onto the spot and rinsing with club soda.

Tip #2: Never have sex with a man who always forgets to give you his home telephone number.

Tip #3: Grate fresh Parmesan cheese by breaking it into small chunks and placing it in your blender on high speed.

Tip #4: Delay sexual gratification of a male suitor by showing him how to use your Thighmaster . . .

Tip #5: Desalt salty soups and stews by adding a chopped potato and a teaspoon of sugar.

ℛomantic ℛoadkill

I no longer want to write this book due to an ugly snafu in my own personal relations with the crankiest mother-fucker to walk the face of the earth. Here I thought I could write a book using myself as the heroine of my own tale, a sort of Judith Krantz novel about how I survived the tarred-over road of love simply by being a well-informed modern gal who cooks. If I sound rather removed from my own situation it is because I am chewing on a Polaroid of my dearly departed in a shirtless— just a minute, please; I have to rip this last piece from my front teeth—now headless yet still waving snapshot from a weekend sex bender the two of us took in Puerto Rico this winter.

This man just poured a little Teflon into the frying

pan of my romantic existence. Our relationship was in his opinion "a nonsticker."

"Christ! Why don't you just poke my eyes out instead?"

Those were the last words I ever said to him. His name is irrelevant since all opportunities for fame, success and true devotional love for him walked out the door with me and my diaphragm. (Or did he walk out the door? Oh shit, it's my book and if I say I walked out the door then that's what happened.)

I see no reason why I have to be gracious about this. In fact, the more blood and gore the better. When I asked him to give me ten good reasons for breaking it off, he responded immediately. As he jammed his Crest toothpaste into his toilet kit he said, "You are so goddamn moody that I never know who's going to open the door. Leona Helmsley? Tammy Faye Bakker? Squeaky Fromme?"

Now I ask you, who's the drama queen here?

"You are hypercritical—you pick on me constantly," he hollered, stuffing his Brooks Brothers suit into his garment bag. "Every little thing I do, you pick, pick, pick."

Once I lightly suggested that if he was going to have sex with me then he had to address me by the right name. *So crucify me.*

"You're this strange cross between a ferocious egomaniac and paranoid, insecure, flipped-out nut." He slithered out the doorway.

Okay, that's enough. I cut him off at item number three because a glutton for punishment I am not. You see, I'm a very sensitive, creative, loving woman who grew up reading *Cosmo*, which told me that I could get out there, sashay in and out of all sorts of sexual relationships while being the aggressive one, and become this sexy, sophisticated, single gal who didn't need anybody. Well, shoot me, I'm from Orange County, California, birthplace of the Richard Nixon Municipal Library, and my circuits have gotten jammed trying to figure exactly what type of woman I am.

You'll have to excuse me, but I'm either having a mood swing or another panic attack. It's hard to tell right now since I am writing with one hand while digging with the other through a stack of assorted snapshots of happier moments in the relationship. I have to retain my artistic eye, since frankly there are a couple of fantastic pictures of me wrapped within the arms of this—wait a minute—now headless, neckless, nameless torso. You know, Polaroids actually taste better than you might think. Unfortunately they lack the salty crunch I yearn for when I am pissed off—and I'm getting more pissed off with each gasping breath. I crave an oily handful of Ruffles potato chips. I want to hear the crunch of my own anger. You will have to excuse me while I go to my kitchen and retrieve a trusty bag. I feel the need to crunch.

I've been gutted like a piece of smoked trout.

The one good thing I can say is that you don't gain weight during this phase of a break-up. Even with all of the influx of junk food, stress and anger tend to make you lose a ton of weight and look like shit. I have never seen a woman eat well during this stage. And why should we? When you are angry, you want to give your feelings a little background music. Try hard, bite-size, crunchy foods that give your anger sound and form; strike back at all of the hurt and anger with food that keeps your jaws clenched. It's the way women allow themselves to feel their anger, by giving it a shape and sound they can respond to—and clamp down upon.

Yes, I did eat the entire bag. I am angry. I can't hear the sound of my own voice so I use crunchy food as my homing pigeon. And don't give me this shit about how a woman can express her anger in the world we live in. She can't. But a woman can be suicidally depressed, which is what everyone prefers because it means that she'll just take her anger out on herself. If I were to act as pissed off as I feel inside, I would be accused of being either hysterical or insane. If a man gets angry, he can yell, he can throw things, he can threaten anybody who crosses his fiery path. But a woman? Well, we bury it in bags of crunchy, bite-size food. See, it's moments like these, when a woman is really hurting, that the world turns on her. It's okay to feel as long as it is not anger or rage, because a display of anger or rage implies that a modern woman is out of control. And control is the key word in defining the persona of the modern woman. But the truth of the matter is that we are out of control because we have no other acceptable way than eating to vent our rage and our anger. *Now pass me the fucking bag of Ruffles this minute.*

FOOD THAT REFLECTS A WOMAN'S ANGER:

Beer nuts
Trail mix
Corn nuts
Honey-roasted nuts
Doritos
Pretzels
Pork rinds
Barbecue potato chips
Cap'n Crunch
Garlic-flavored croutons
Popcorn
Rice cakes
Granola bars
Wheat thins
Carrots
Celery
Any Jolly Rancher hard
    candies
Lemon drops
Sweet Tarts
Hot Tamales
Jaw Breakers
Bite-size Butterfingers
Every style of Pepperidge
    Farm cookies
Ice
Polaroid pictures

Although eating hard, crunchy food is the way a woman most often expresses her anger, it still gets swallowed up inside her. But that is where the craving for crunchy food comes from—the need to assert herself when a woman feels powerless. I can't assert myself within the context of a modern relationship because my lovers just walk away. Promises that were made have been broken without explanation. It's over. That's it. With modern sex there is no place in a relationship for a woman to effectively assert her expectations. Relationships come and go so quickly these days that they get jumbled together. Things you should have said to the previous lover you are now screaming at the present one. Whatever feelings aren't being buried into food are being thrown onto the next relationship.

I always say the two greatest cooks to get friendly with during this time are Mrs. Sara Lee. (Is Sara Lee married? Well, they make everybody who acts in television commercials wear wedding rings, I guess, to imply that they are more reliable and trustworthy people to be associated with. The only actors advertisers don't like to wear wedding rings are those dopey sluts on beer ads and radial tire commercials—I know there is a big message in there somewhere, but I am not going to figure it out because those dopey sluts look a hell of a lot happier than I am right now, so screw 'em.) Now, getting back to my original suggestion of good cooks to know: Señor Frito Lay. If you ask me, Señor Lay is a very instinctive guy who makes food that so many people crave when they are angry. He has developed food that makes you feel sick after eating, but you wake up craving the next day. *Now that is talent.*

(I know this doesn't have anything to do with anything but since we are on the topic of television commercials, I'd just like to say that I think Juan Valdez, you know, the Colombian Coffee guy with the donkey and

sombrero? Yeah, him. I think he looks like a public mas-
turbator. If I saw some guy hanging around my super-
market aisles giving me that horny lip curl with that
smelly donkey I'd call the store manager. Immediately. I
just had to get that off my chest. Consider that your first
clever cook's shopping tip.)

I have another problem. You see, I accidentally
dumped all of my girlfriends when I started seeing the
hairless bastard. I didn't mean to, I swear to God. It's just
that I get carried away in romance sometimes and I blow
people off for a while. But what else can I say? It was
unbridled love. . . . When I saw him sitting across from
me at Sally Lynn Fisher's dinner party, he put me into a
lulu of a love trance. There he was, glossy brown hair
with big reindeer eyes and a smile that could unlock your
front door. "Would you care for some Mylanta?" he inquired after Sally Lynn made the salmonella announce-
ment over cake and coffee. I just sighed and drank the
entire bottle. It was curtains from that moment on. I called
my girlfriend Evie from Sally Lynn's bedroom to tell her
that I had met the finest example of walking testosterone
I had ever laid eyes upon. "Junie, now just get a grip on
yourself and don't you dare." Who knows what Evie said
next because he walked into the bedroom to get his coat
and I dropped the phone on the floor. "Junie? Junie, are
you still there? . . . Junie? . . . Junie, are you okay?" Evie's
voice rattled from under the bed. "Is someone calling
your name?" he asked, smiling like he had one hour to
live. "Who gives a shit?" I said. We left Sally Lynn Fisher's
apartment and that was the last time I talked to Sally
Lynn, Evie, Sharon, my mother, my cleaning woman . . .

Now I have to find a way to get Evie to talk to me
again. She's a great friend. You always need a girlfriend
who has been single for a while to help you find your
balance. They possess that air of detachment that you
don't, and they can see the situation from a less emotional

slant, thus can bring character flaws into the light more quickly. (But hell, it's not like I was going to listen to a word she would say anyway, so maybe it's good I haven't talked to her in a while.) It's best to have girlfriends who understand when you go off on a romantic seizure. Because there is nothing worse than a girlfriend who rubs your face in it when the seizure is over. So I am taking me, my greasy blue bag of Ruffles and my pink fluffy bunny slippers on a walk across Central Park so I can throw myself at Evie's feet and beg for her to be my friend again.

Hang on a minute. I need my sunny yellow raincoat.

"You slept with *him* on the first date, didn't you?" Evie's voice blared through the speaker in the lobby of her apartment building.

"I absolutely did not." (I did, but my mother will be reading this book and I don't want her to know.) "Now will you please buzz me in so I can come up and talk to you about what has happened?" I yelled back into the speaker.

"You are lying and I'm not buzzing you in until you tell me the truth," Evie hissed.

"I didn't have sex with *him*, but I saw *it* a couple of times that night. Now will you shut up and let me in your goddamn apartment building!" I hollered, noticing the crowd of people gathering around me.

I won. She buzzed me in.

"I have no sympathy for you," Evie stated as she opened her front door, licking a cherry popsicle.

"Oh, shut up. Like you haven't rolled a hundred guys on the first date? Don't you start crying virgin to me, Evie."

I hate it when Evie gets that strappy tone in her voice. You see, Evie is a commodities broker who wakes up every morning and drinks a cup of glass shards with

Sweet 'N Low for breakfast. She's pretty too, which is a problem when you're a gal who wears No Nonsense pantyhose. Evie's sort of an Eastern bloc version of Joan Collins—voluptuous, lips stained with Chanel's Sun Fire Red, lots of tight black leather with gold buttons, Versace-style. A true native New Yorker. When it comes to men, Evie ain't got time for creeps, perverts, or morons. At thirty-eight she's done the circuit—the married man, the pork belly broker from Biloxi, the gynecologist on Seventy-Third and Park and the United Parcel delivery man. A true socialist when it comes to men.

These days Evie is like the resident born-again virgin. Six months ago she met Sol, a mortgage bank financier —a two-pack-a-day Camel non-filter-type of guy—who filed for bankruptcy twice in the '80s. He's the type of guy God loves: a sinner in need of a lot of forgiveness, a sort of Jewish John Gotti. "Whatever . . . I don't need gory details," is Sol's answer to everything. He isn't into probing the universe to find the totality of his essence. Just a dry gin martini with two olives, please. Happiness to Sol is cooking his woman a peppery steak au poivre with plenty of lightly salted shoe-string fried potatoes and a salad made of iceberg lettuce with slivers of purple cabbage and hunks of bleu cheese (which is to be served after the main course, European-style). He's like the Cary Grant of Brooklyn Heights, with plenty of musky after-shave and diamond pinky rings on both hands. Sol's a great guy to know if you owe a lot of money around town. If you had a bad cold, Sol's the type of person who'd cough up his right lung to make you feel better. No Hallmark cards from this guy.

(Sol's steak au poivre is really delicious because he sears two eight-ounce fillets in butter and crushed black peppercorns, then he quickly adds low-fat sour cream, mustard, beef juices and a shot of Wild Turkey—he started using Wild Turkey after filing for his second bankruptcy. Most traditional recipes call for heavy cream and Cognac, but I am tellin' you, his steaks are succulent and tender and his cream sauce has a delightful little tang to it. For his shoestring potatoes he does something very interesting. He takes two large Idaho potatoes—unpeeled —slices them into thin strips, rinses them in cold water and pats them dry on a paper towel. Next he rubs them very lightly in 3 or 4 tablespoons of olive oil and bakes them on a cookie sheet in a preheated 450-degree oven, turning after fifteen minutes, with a total baking time of thirty minutes. Sol's fries are light, crispy morsels that taste wonderful with a quick dash of garlic salt.)

"Spare me the details on this one, will you?" Evie pleaded. "And I hope you weren't combing the streets in that getup you've got on. You look like you've just come from an exorcism," Evie said as she flopped onto the couch.

"Don't you want to know how awful he was to me?" I cried, shoving her stupid schnauzer Lucky off my spot on the couch. "And how do you expect me to look? I've just been romantically harpooned, for Christ's sake."

"Be nice to that dog or you are out on the streets again. You dumped all of your friends the moment you met this guy," Evie said as she bounced Lucky on her lap.

"I just thought—" I said yanking the tiger print pillow out from under Lucky's furry chin.

"*No*, you did *not* think, you just jumped in face first. We had a long discussion about this two weeks before you met this guy. Remember when you said you were going to be more protective of yourself? Didn't you tell Sol and me over dinner at Elaine's in November that your values had changed and you were taking a *new* approach to your relationships?" Evie said walking into the kitchen.

"Hey girlie-girl," Sol yelled from the kitchen. "You

want to stay and have dinner with Evie Bug and me? I'm fixing chicken 'n dumplings tonight."

"She's heartbroken again, Sol. Talk to her, will you?" Evie said pouring a glass of red wine.

"Isn't anyone going to offer me a drink?" I whined. "Stop growling at me, Lucky."

"Get her a Coke with two limes will ya, Sol? No booze, Junie. You have got to promise me, *no booze*," Evie ordered while she set the dining room table.

"Girlie-girl, it's a jungle out there. Ya gotta take your time and become a smart zoo keeper or your prey is gonna turn on you. Find yourself a nice guy. Ya know, someone who doesn't want to be on '*STAR SEARCH*,' " Sol said, stirring my Coke with a green naked-lady swizzle stick.

"Are you staying for dinner or not?" Evie asked.

"I'll sit with you, but I'm not going to eat. I can't. I hurt too much." I started to cry.

"Look Junie, you know as well as I do that before I met Sol, I fucked every guy that walked through my front door. Jesus, I can remember back in the Studio 54 days —all booze and drugs and crazy shit. I was freaked out all the time with all these weird guys who would call me late at night and ask if they could drop over for a while. I wouldn't even remember who they were. I used to live on Hot Tamales and Excedrin PM. I was obsessed with guys who didn't have the decency to return my phone calls. By the time they did, it was too late. I was already broken. I had taken the pregnancy test *alone*. I found out what that little rash was all about *alone*. By the time Sol came around I was this brittle, ball-busting bitch—wasn't I, Sol?" Evie yelled into the kitchen.

My eyes are fixated on Evie's feet right now. She flap-flaps as she cuts through the white shag carpet wearing gold rhinestone sandals. Evie flaps quickly across the room with her blood-red toenails marking her path. Flap-

flap go her jaws as she flaps into the kitchen to talk to Sol. Everything about her flaps quickly—her gold twinkling sandals, her leopard print stretch pants with matching sweater—like a low flapping thunder. There's an intensity about her that is well staged and directed. She flaps crisp and clean with a biting sting when she's frustrated or pissed off. Evie can flap with her jaws and flap with her feet while she slaps on another ring of lipstick. An incredibly modern gal.

Walking out of the kitchen Sol planted a bowl of minted peas on the table. "Breaks my heart to think of you back then, doll. You were like a flower with all its petals yanked off."

Evie flaps over to him and kisses him on the cheek. "Yeah, but you helped me to put my petals back on, didn't you, Sol?"

"Whatever, doll. I was just so bamboozled by you. You were fabulous. A no bullshitsky type of gal. No tricks, no rah-rah. I'd had my fill of that type of broad," Sol said as he sat down at the table, tucking a zebra print polyester napkin into the neck of his shirt.

If you were to meet them separately you would never put the two of them together. Sol's rhythm is much slower than Evie's snappy flap. He sort of lumbers around the room like the furniture is a bit too small and delicate to welcome his heavy plop into the banana leaf seats. Don't get me wrong. It is not that he is fat, he's just too large for Evie's jungle cruise, overpriced, Arabian nights disco-style decor. You know what I mean? Not everyone looks good in animal prints.

"Hey, doll, we gotta get something that I can sit in. You know, something that doesn't have fangs comin' out of wood."

Now, I am not crazy for Sol's Chicken 'n Dumplings. He uses the backs and necks of frying chickens, which are gross if you ask me—too many baby bones popping out everywhere and very little juicy white meat. It would break his heart if he knew that I had said this about his mother's recipe, but I like to use juicy, meaty drumsticks and thighs lightly dusted in peppered flour, browned for a few minutes and simmered in chicken stock. Sol makes his own chicken stock, which is a waste of time. Just buy the canned stuff, it's fine. Add chunks of carrots, celery, white onions and a big handful of dried sage and thyme leaves and simmer for half an hour. Before I make the dumplings, I remove all chicken and vegetables, leaving only the broth to thicken. Then after the dumplings have simmered for about fifteen minutes or so I add the chicken and vegetables.

Serve this dish with some Swiss chard and spinach sautéed in chopped garlic, olive oil and lemon juice and get yourself ready for a religious experience. If you are going to use frozen Swiss chard and spinach then use this trick: Allow it to thaw either by microwave (2 to 3 minutes) or lightly steam in a pot with a vegetable steamer for 5 to 7 minutes. Once defrosted, strain out all water and sauté. Since you have not cooked but only defrosted them, the leaves are still tender firm and will not taste overcooked like most frozen vegetables. Remember this trick whenever you are using frozen vegetables—defrost, drain and sauté.

See, it is easier for me to talk about a goddamn recipe than it is for me to reveal my own feelings about the breakup with that spineless prick. If Evie wasn't here to shed some light on my tortured situation, I have no idea where I would be right now. My emotions are tangled into one giant knot and I have lost my voice because it's buried underneath a mountain of stale potato chips. That is what I do: I channel my anger back into myself with food.

Is it that I am angry with myself for sleeping with someone who makes me feel like I don't have a right to want some commitment? Is it that I am angry at myself for desperately looking for closeness in men who don't give it to me? Am I angry that I can't trust myself to know who it is I should get involved with? I cannot honestly tell you which one of these feelings is the one that tears me to shreds inside. Evie helps me to take responsibility for the fact that I slept with him before I was ready. The loins were ready, but the girl was not. I fooled myself into thinking I was and repeated the mistake of using sex to get to know someone. But it never works.

The fact of the matter is that I see myself as being far more sophisticated than I actually am, but I am not a casual woman. Why, there isn't a casual bone in my entire body. With casual sex you touch flesh with numbed fingers. It's intense and distant in the same breath. I think men view sex with a renewed sense of virility and women see it as a hallmark of our sexual liberation. But liberation from what? Our feelings, our instincts, our history as nurturers? That's why the phrase "casual sex" is just one giant mind fuck if you ask me. A weenie roast at the beach is casual, but sex? Well, it has never felt like a weenie roast to me.

I have to rely on Evie to be my voice of sanity until I find my own. Evie has been on the high seas of modern love, so when she talks, I listen. I had almost forgotten about those years before Sol. Evie was a very different woman. She was high strung and angry most of the time. (Kind of like I am now.) I met Evie the first week I moved to the Big Apple. She was making lots of money back then and we'd order a limo and hit the town. Nothing intimidated Evie except for the guys she slept with. We'd go to Mr. Chow's or La Cote Basque or maybe The "21" Club. Instead of eating the meals we had ordered, we'd pop breath mints and futz with our hair. Looking good in a red leather booth is crucial in this town.

Once we were dining at "21" and Evie ran into a guy

she had had a fling with around Christmastime the year before. We spotted him in the bar trying to seduce a miniature bust of the Statue of Liberty. He had that look, like he had spent too many hours under the tanning lamps— lizard-like, with a tiny pink forked tongue.

"Ah . . . hi. I think we know each other, don't we?" he said, swaggering over, wearing a bold houndstooth-check wool suit.

"No, I'm sorry, I don't think we do. Are you a broker?" Evie said with a nervous glance.

"Ah, gee, no I'm not a broker. I think we met at a Christmas party at Michael Roper's loft. . . . Your name is Edie, right?" He pulled on his gold-hooked lapis cuff links.

"I think you've got the wrong girl," she said, rubbing her lips with her right index finger.

"I don't think so . . . but if you want to be that way . . . then I guess we don't know each other." He shook his head as he strutted off, slapping our waiter on the back.

Evie and I returned to our baked potatoes and said nothing.

(This may not be the time to bring this up, but baked potatoes are never a good thing to order in a restaurant. Most restaurants steam bake them which results in a soggy, dense, mealy, starchy mush. To get baked potatoes with a crispy skin and fluffy center it's best to bake them in a preheated 400-degree oven for 45 to 50 minutes for a medium to large potato, 6 to 8 ounces. The secret to retaining a fluffy center is to pierce the potato, a few minutes after baking, using the tines of a dinner fork. Lightly press down the middle of the potato and then across. Next, press the ends of the potato with your fingertips—use hot pads—and push on the ends toward the center. The meat, or white fluffy part, will push up from the skin and will look like those potatoes do in television commercials. I just thought you might want to know that.)

"So why'd you pretend not to know him?" I asked, watching her jab at her potato.

"Because, what is there left to say? I mean, should I make him feel okay about the fact that he didn't bother to call me, even though he had invited me to go to St. Bart's with him for New Year's? We spent all of Christmas with each other and I'm supposed to be the one that makes it okay? It's not okay—on any level." She twitched, squeezing another slice of lemon onto her potato.

"Maybe he had a girlfriend or something. Maybe he . . ." I said, waving my fork in the air.

"Yeah, maybe he was involved . . . maybe he's gay . . . maybe he's a guy who wears three thousand dollar suits and walks like a nice guy and talks like a nice guy and smells like a nice guy, but when it comes down to it, sex is just something he pads his ego with. I felt like I did something wrong—like I wasn't sexy enough or I had told him too much about myself. . . . I can't eat this thing. I put too much lemon on it. Let's get a pack of cigarettes from the waiter," she sighed, letting her fork drop onto the plate.

Evie understands the powerlessness that I feel in my pursuit for love. She too knows what it feels like to get all caught up in the love swoon, only to feel betrayed one more time. Evie felt so betrayed by herself and her search for sensual love, that she would often break out into quiet, hopeless tears when she was alone with herself. She felt powerless and out of control. Through her feelings I can see my own. I am unable to allow myself some feeling of security and trust in my life as a single woman and it makes me very angry. See, I turn on myself for not knowing better, for not being more in control, for not being able to connect with the instinctive reflex of my feminine strength—my ability to nurture from within.

I threw that away when I went in search of love through a casual relationship. But when I think of Evie and those nights she spent alone pulling herself back together, I understand that I need to spend some time alone so I can learn to value what lies deep in my heart. I laugh as I write about the bloody recipes in this chapter. For me to pick up my ass and go cook for myself would mean that I had found enough self-esteem to want to feed myself. Until I am really ready to be totally alone, I am going to use hard, crunchy food to hold back the pain. Is it really HIM I am longing for? No. That much I can tell you. The person I am longing for is myself.

This may sound like a strange thing to remember, but whenever I think of a woman with no sense of self I think of Evie's refrigerator before she met Sol. I can tell what is going on in a woman's psyche by what she keeps in her refrigerator. (Most people snoop in medicine chests, which usually have a bad array of legal drugs from Walgreen's.) When I opened Evie's I discovered the following contents:

4 bottles of Chanel nail polish
3 pairs of Christian Dior pantyhose
1 package of Eveready batteries
1 can of Slimfast
½ can of Diet Coke
1 empty package of peanut M&M's

I will save the best for last: 1 pair of Timberland hiking boots—the left boot in the vegetable bin, the right boot in the fruit bin. A refrigerator like this tells me that this is a woman who doesn't know how to feed herself. Once I saw her heat up a can of cat food and serve it to Lucky.

My refrigerator isn't really a good example because I am always testing out recipes. Even though I have no self-esteem or self whatsoever, I cook for other people and eat Cheetos while standing in front of the refrigerator because I really do not know how to take care of myself. I can cook, but that doesn't mean that I know how to feed myself. Meals to me are usually spent sticking my head into the fridge and poking my nose into assorted sizes of Tupperware containers. The contents are always mysteriously stiff and lifeless. I pick at each bite with tiny claw-like grabs and stand encased in white refrigerated light while I give myself just enough mouthfuls to survive. Never enough to really live, but merely to survive. The only thing I taste is coldness, which keeps my guts nicely chilled. I don't feel safe enough to allow a thaw. I'm afraid my rage might swallow me up. That is why I wound up where I am one more time. What I feel at this moment reminds me of a poem I read some time ago.

AUTOBIOGRAPHY IN FIVE CHAPTERS

CHAPTER 1

I walk down the street. There is a hole in the sidewalk. I fall in. It feels like I will never get out.

CHAPTER 2

I walk down the street. There is a hole in the sidewalk. I fall in. It takes forever to get out.

CHAPTER 3

I walk down the street. There is a hole in the sidewalk. I fall in. I get out immediately.

CHAPTER 4

I walk down the street. There is a hole in the sidewalk. I walk around it.

CHAPTER 5

I walk down a new street.

Anonymous

It seems that I can never get past Chapter Two.

But Evie walks down a new street today and her

story is what keeps me going right now. I knew the day she let me past her frozen smile that she trusted me enough to let me see her unspeakable loneliness. Her hopeless smile that day gave our friendship the compassion it needed to begin to melt away the isolation between Evie and the rest of the world. I was the first person to meet Evie's sorrow.

To view Evie as a stranger back then, you would see a woman who was beautiful, extremely successful, hard driving and totally independent, who didn't need anyone or anything. She was the type of success story that would make Helen Gurly Brown proud. Any pleasurable activity that she did for herself was about putting together a more alluring package. The frantic aerobics classes (I don't know if I would consider that a pleasurable activity), the brain-suffocating cut, perm and blow dry sessions at the hair salon, the ceremonial French tip manicure, the bone crushing facials, and the satan-invoking lip and bikini wax were all about Evie fixing herself.

After the Thing ended with the guy in the houndstooth suit, she had a Thing with a UPS delivery guy. (A Thing is not a relationship and it's not a one night stand, yet you've been sexual so it's no longer considered dating—it's that Thing in between, that place where you have no rights to expectations or boundaries or commitments. That's a Thing.) The Thing with the delivery guy was especially frustrating. Evie didn't know if she could depend on him or even know what she should expect from their Thing, and it made her crave those giant-size turquoise blue Jaw Breakers. (You know, those candies thirteen-year-old boys gnaw on after school to abate their imploding libidos?) But all of her Things had left her feeling angry and frustrated about sleeping with men who didn't want to know her after the weekend ended. Evie never wanted a Thing, she wanted a relationship. She is an aggressive, impatient woman who goes after whatever she wants. Patience is something Evie didn't have time to schedule in her Filofax.

"I don't know what is wrong with me. At work, I can feel a deal is good in my gut. Whenever I check my gut about a guy, I feel like the mercury in a thermometer, but I can't get a reading because the cold steely feelings push up and up. I feel nervous and panicky in my gut, and the mercury pushes and pushes up into my neck and jaws. Then it's like all that grey, icy fluid explodes in the middle of my brain and I put my head down on my pillow and cry. Alone. It happens every time I meet someone I'm attracted to. It's like a warning about something, as if I'm going to get mangled by something. I don't know if it's the guy or all of the rage I feel from betraying myself all these years."

(Now I crave a live rat right now so I can rip its head off—that's what would help me cope. As a woman coming off the heels of a major breakup, I should feed myself a plate of warm food. I just can't. For me to care for myself right now would mean I'd have to face my rage. I will not lie to you. I have not even begun to tap into my rage. It is choking me. It will take some time for me to find the courage to face the fact that at this moment I am a woman with no sense of self. If I had a sense of self I would not feel so trapped within my feelings. I have to look toward my friendship with Evie to see what it is I need to do for myself. I need a type of insight that I am sorely lacking.)

Evie got smart in her relationships. She made a very conscious decision to stop dating entirely until she could trust her instincts again. "I'm not screwing anyone until I know who he is and I believe what he says to me. My Japanese clients are very smart. They hang back and see if you return their phone calls on time and study how you treat people. They act slowly, never hurrying to get a deal done. I'm going to apply this tactic with the guys I meet and I'm going to stand back and check out the integrity of their words and actions."

Not long after our conversation, Evie went back to night school to get her masters in art history. When she wasn't working, she was studying and going to class. I didn't see much of her during that time—no one did. Evie focused and cleared her head. When she cried she knew what she was crying about: She was terrified she would always feel swallowed up by this tortured longing for some love and respect. She used to always call it her "cry of the heart." "My tears are the sweat from my soul trying to stand up, Junie. I'm crying so I can stand up and have some self-respect." When she said this to me, I had no idea what she was talking about and I think she wanted to punch me in the kazoo. I'm afraid I was not much comfort. "Evie, why don't you just take five Midols and see if that helps." Evie then looked at me as only Evie can. "I can't wait till you get hit with some of this stuff, 'cause sometimes, Junie, you are such a stupid ass."

From time to time I would fax Evie recipes for things she could make while studying. She wasn't going out for business dinners anymore and wanted casserole recipes that she could heat up when she got home at night. "I don't want to become a gourmet chef. I just want simple things that will keep during the week." I saw Evie start to feed herself and her anger began to lift.

The rebirth of a clever cook.

Evie met Sol in the Registrar's Office at Hunter College. Sol began talking to her as he was registering for a class in auto painting and detailing. (He ruined his reputation on Wall Street and needed a skill that would get him a steady job.) She didn't like him at first. After she finished the meeting with her counselor, she found him sitting in a metal folding chair waiting for her. Sol walked her to the subway and asked her to meet him for coffee the following week. Edie refused to give him her telephone number and took his instead. For months they would meet for coffee and then Sol would ride the subway with her to make sure she got home safely. He told her it worried him that she rode the trains at night by herself. Sol was the first man to remember Evie's birthday.

The first time they made love, Sol was worried he might have a heart attack. He told her he hadn't had sex with a woman since his wife left him right after the first bankruptcy years before. Evie told Sol that if they were going to have sex, he would have to stay and not leave her alone, wondering if she had made herself too vulnerable again. Sol promised Evie that he wouldn't leave her alone and she promised Sol that she would take care of him if he had a heart attack during their lovemaking. Sol moved in with Evie soon after that night.

I can obviously see that I am going to have to put myself on ice for a while and chill out. I have no inner foundation and it shows . . . in my relationships, in how I take care of myself, in how I cope, in the choices I make. I have committed the clever cook's fatal flaw: I have lost my instincts, and it forces me to become dependent on men like Frito Lay. The first step in my own survival is to acknowledge that I am an emotional nomad who has just slept with another wandering camel. Our love was like an oasis—always looming on the horizon, yet never any water or deck chairs. I long for someone I don't even know, but who I have made love with—a strange notion when you think about it, to long for someone who you don't even know. I have to find a better way to assert myself. I have to have a sense of myself. I have to change, and the idea overwhelms me. I realize that what little dignity I once felt for myself, I have lost. I'm in deeper shit than I originally thought I was in. . . .

To encourage me to cook after the end of a Thing would be cruel and inhuman. Evie violently disagrees with me on this point, but screw her. If you can find the inspiration to squeeze a healthy mouthful of Cheez Wiz onto a Ritz cracker, consider it a sign that soon you will become a clever cook. (And that you will survive.) I wish I felt inspired to whip up a great anger-gnashing recipe for China-roasted almonds. They are delicious, relatively healthy and very easy to make. Basically all you have to do is marinate them for a couple of hours in soy sauce, drain all liquid and roast them on a cookie sheet in a preheated 350-degree oven for 10 to 12 minutes. To prevent burning the almonds—which is an easy thing to do when you're pissed off—jostle the cookie sheet every couple of minutes. This will also help prevent sticking. China-roasted almonds are delicious on salads or any breakfast cereal or just eaten by the handful. I am so angry right now that there is no way I could make any China-roasted nuts. The only nuts I want to roast are his. (If I remember, I will include an unbelievable recipe for a cold broccoli salad with China-roasted almonds in a spicy ginger dressing that is mind bending it's so good. It's also great served warm on steamed brown rice.) I gave this recipe to Evie during her pre-Sol days. Since Evie is by nature a clever cook, she adds chopped tofu or shredded chicken to this dish. But I'm getting ahead of myself here. Let's face it, I am too fucked up to steam any broccoli right now.

While Evie and Sol were scraping the leftover chicken 'n' dumplings into Tupperware, I went into their bedroom and called Him to see if we could talk. I got his answering machine, which told me to "Have a nice day." I hung up without leaving a message, covered my face with Evie's pillow and screamed into it until I heard Lucky yipping hysterically in the living room—drowned out by a bloody schnauzer.

"Do you want to sleep on our couch tonight?" Evie commanded as she stood in the doorway of her bedroom.

"No, I won't be able to sleep. I'll just keep you all up," I said, pulling myself up from the bed.

"Then go home and cry, and listen to yourself. You'll be all right, Junie, but you got to give yourself some time. And listen to yourself. Nothing is going to change until you do."

"I'm tired, Evie, I am very, very tired. All I want to do is sleep until I forget what he looks like."

"Hey, Junie, what you need is to wake up. That's what you need."

Life sucks.

I hate his guts.

I should have never slept with him on the first date.
—JUNIE

Sol's Mama's Chicken 'n' Dumplings

SERVES 3 TO 4

The Stock

4 tablespoons olive oil
2 cloves garlic, minced
1 yellow onion, chopped
2 stalks celery, chopped
3 carrots, chopped
4 each of chicken thighs
     and drumsticks

½ cup white wine
4 12-ounce cans chicken
     stock
2 teaspoons dried thyme
1 bay leaf
1 teaspoon dried sage
1 bunch parsley, chopped

Pour the olive oil into a large stock pot and sauté garlic and onions on medium heat until translucent. Add celery, carrots and chicken and continue to sauté for about 5 minutes. Add the wine and the chicken stock along with the thyme, bay leaf and sage and bring to a rapid boil for 45 minutes. With a large slotted spoon, remove the chicken and allow it to cool until you can remove the skin and bones. Return the chicken meat to pot and add the parsley. Lower the heat to a slow simmer and cover with a lid while you make the dumplings.

Sol's Dumplings

2½ cups unbleached
  flour
4 teaspoons baking
  powder
1 teaspoon salt

3 tablespoons butter, cut
  into pieces
1 tablespoon chopped
  parsley
1¼ cups milk

Mix together the flour, baking powder and salt in a medium mixing bowl. Cut in the butter and blend using your fingers or a fork until the mixture has a grainy texture. Add the parsley and milk and stir until just blended. Do not overmix. Dumplings should have a grainy and lumpy texture.

Using a large serving spoon, drop the dumpling mixture into the simmering chicken stock and let simmer with the lid off for about 5 minutes. Then cover and continue to simmer for another 15 to 20 minutes, or until dumplings cook to twice their original size.

Sol's Steak au Poivre

SERVES 2 TO 3

2 tablespoons black
   peppercorns
3 or 4 small tenderloin
   steaks (1 pound total
   weight)
2 tablespoons butter
1 tablespoon lemon juice
1 tablespoon Worcester-
   shire sauce

2 tablespoons low-fat sour
   cream
1 tablespoon chopped
   parsley
4 tablespoons Wild Turkey
   bourbon

Grind the whole peppercorns in blender or coffee grinder
(but be prepared to never use your coffee grinder for
coffee again; better just to buy coarsely ground black
pepper or crush peppercorns using wax paper and a rolling pin). Rub peppercorns into both sides of the steak
and set aside.

In a small saucepan melt the butter, then add the
lemon juice, Worcestershire sauce, sour cream and
chopped parsley. Sauté until bubbling hot. Set aside.

Broil the steaks for approximately 2½ minutes on
each side as close as you can to the broiler flame for a
rare to medium-rare steak. To cook the steaks on the
stove, sprinkle a heavy skillet with salt and heat on high
flame until the pan gets smokey hot. Reduce to medium
heat, add the steaks and cook for 3 to 4 minutes on each
side for a rare to medium-rare steak.

Add the Wild Turkey to the sauce and light a match
to it to burn out the alcohol or flambé. Pour the sauce
over steaks and serve.

58

Oven-Fried Shoestring Potatoes

SERVES 2 TO 3

4 medium Russet or Idaho potatoes, scrubbed and dried

⅓ cup olive oil
1 tablespoon kosher or sea salt

Preheat oven to 450 degrees. Cut the potatoes into thin strips. (Soak them in cold water to prevent browning if you are preparing them ahead of time; dry potatoes thoroughly using paper towels.) Place the potato on a cookie sheet, making sure that none overlap. Thoroughly coat with the olive oil and sprinkle with the salt. Bake for 50 minutes or until crispy brown. When done to your liking, drain on paper towels and sprinkle lightly with garlic salt before serving.

Sol's Sautéed Swiss Chard and Spinach in Lemon and Garlic

SERVES 2 TO 3

1 9-ounce package of fro-
zen Swiss chard,
thawed and drained
1 9-ounce package of fro-
zen spinach, thawed
and drained

2 tablespoons olive oil
2 cloves garlic, minced
2 tablespoons lemon juice
Salt and pepper to taste

Thaw and completely drain all water from Swiss chard and spinach. Leaving water in Swiss chard and spinach will make them soggy and flavorless.

In a saucepan, heat the olive oil and sauté the garlic until golden brown. Add Swiss chard and spinach leaves and cook, over medium heat, for 3 to 4 minutes stirring continuously. Add the lemon juice, salt and pepper and serve.

Broccoli-Almond Salad

SERVES 3 TO 4

¾ cup raw whole
 almonds
⅓ cup soy sauce
3 to 3½ cups broccoli
 florets with ½ inch
 stems

Spicy Ginger Dressing
(recipe follows)

Preheat the oven to 350 degrees. In a small mixing bowl, marinate the almonds in the soy sauce for at least 1 hour.

Wash and trim the broccoli, saving the florets and cutting the stems into ½-inch rounds. Put the broccoli in a steaming basket and place it in a saucepan filled with 1 inch of water. Cover and steam the broccoli for 3 to 4 minutes, or until tender but still crunchy. To retain bright green color, fill a medium mixing bowl with ice cubes and water. Immerse the steamed broccoli in the water bath for 1 minute, then drain and set aside.

Drain the almonds, reserving the soy sauce. Place the almonds on a baking sheet and toast for approximately 12 minutes, stirring the almonds every few minutes to prevent burning. Remove from the oven and allow to cool. (Toasted soy almonds are great to serve with cocktails too!) Make the dressing and toss it with the steamed broccoli. Add almonds just before serving.

Broccoli can be served either hot or cold. If making ahead of time (and I wouldn't make it more than a day ahead), don't pour the dressing onto the broccoli until just before serving. Dressing may discolor broccoli and make it turn a little gray—gross.

Spicy Ginger Dressing

¼ cup balsamic vinegar
½ cup olive oil
2 tablespoons Dijon
    mustard

1 tablespoon soy sauce
1 clove garlic, minced
Salt and pepper to taste
1 T ginger

Combine all the ingredients and store in an air-tight container.

Note: Evie used to marinate cubed tofu or shredded chicken in this dressing before she'd toss it with the broccoli. She'd also make up a little brown rice, using chicken stock instead of water, toss the whole mess together and eat it hot while in her jammies and sitting in front of her television set. This is a great salad served hot or cold. I am sure you will think up other great variations.

From the Desk of Evie Young

Re: Tips for a Clever Cook's Pantry
To: Any Beginning Clever Cook

Dear Readers:
I hope the following list will come in handy. Junie was supposed to do it, but she is probably sobbing in some gutter right now. Anyway, these are some things I find very useful to have on hand when I am too tired or too depressed to run to the corner market. Trust me, getting clobbered like this is the best thing that could have ever happened to Junie. It's time she grew up.

Hope we meet under happier circumstances,

Evie Louise Young

SUGGESTED PANTRY LIST:

Bisquick
brownie mix
pudding mix
cornbread mix
crushed canned
    tomatoes
stewed tomatoes
tomato paste
tomato sauce
canned broth, chicken
    and beef
canned soups,
    assorted selections
tuna fish
smoked oysters
anchovy fillets
artichoke hearts
assorted pasta
assorted rice
olives
assorted nuts and
    dried fruits
capers
jams and jellies
honey
peanut butter
apple cider vinegar
white wine vinegar
red wine vinegar
balsamic vinegar
soy sauce
crackers

barbecue sauce
Dijon mustard
kidney beans
garbanzo beans
corned beef hash
popcorn
assorted canned
    vegetables
decaf coffee
cereal
salad dressing
white onions
club soda
olive oil
corn oil
baking soda
baking powder
ketchup
pickles
pickle relish
assorted teas
horseradish sauce
Tabasco sauce
Worcestershire sauce
baking potatoes
white sugar
brown sugar—light
    and dark
powdered sugar
white flour
vanilla extract

In Bed . . . Alone

I haven't spoken to anyone in months.

Except Alana, the psychic from Brooklyn, who normally does not take on clients over the phone unless they possess two outstanding qualities: a purple iridescent aura that radiates two and a half inches from the physical body, and a Visa card.

When I asked her what color my aura was, she responded, "You have a brassy yellow aura that is weak in radiating qualities. This doesn't look good," she added, getting ready to hang up on me.

"Oh, wait . . . well, that's totally explainable. I haven't gotten any highlights in months so you must be zeroing in on the base color of my hair," I said as I popped my head up from my fluffy goose-down comforter.

"Wait a minute," she said, "I am receiving new information here. You have an approval code rating of twenty-seven, which is numerologically good because two plus seven equals nine, and nine is a completion number. This is very good," she said in a phony Greco-Roman accent.

Shoving another handful of barbecue potato chips into my mouth, I inquired, "You mean to tell me that you have to have an approval code rating to talk to God?"

"You do when you're talking to him with an out-of-state Visa card," she replied.

"Hmm . . . Can you tell me what you see for me in the future?" I pleaded, snapping off the Home Shopping Club with my remote.

"I see . . . a man who is sobbing into his hands. He is sitting on a mossy rock somewhere in a forest. He is calling out for you," she hummed.

(Now that's weird. A mossy rock . . . maybe a mossy office chair somewhere down on Wall Street . . . but a rock in a forest? Maybe her psychic satellite dish is picking up on *Robin Hood*, which is playing on HBO this weekend. Do you suppose that Kevin Costner is sobbing for me on some rock in a forest?)

"Well, what I am seeing is the point the two of you separated in a previous life. He was a trapper in Wyoming back then, and you were the wife of a traveling minister. When your caravan pulled into town, he came to one of your husband's revivals, where the two of you met and had a wild, passionate affair in the back of your wagon train," she said as her bracelets clanged against the phone.

"Oh . . . well, then that obviously must be us. I slept with him on the first date back then too. Was it true love?" I asked, urgently pulling my matted hair out of my face.

"Well, let me see here . . . I'm receiving more new information . . . It seems that he left you and ran off into the woods to fetch animal skins for his people, leaving you worried about being pregnant with his child." She stopped to take a sip from her drink—Scotch probably.

"Jesus, he got me pregnant? Did he come back for me and the child, or was he torn limb from limb by a herd of wild boars?"

"Well, no. It seems that you were already impregnated by a barker from the livestock auction in the previous town. You were a very desperate woman, since your parents traded you for two pigs and a plough when you were thirteen years old. . . . Hang on, I've got another call coming in," she snorted.

(Holy God . . . I don't know what's worse, the fact that I was whoring around with every man with a dick in the entire wild west or the fact that my parents, those people who I have loved and trusted my entire life, bartered me for two lousy pigs and a plough. I wonder if that's why they haven't called me lately; they know I know.)

"Okay, now, we've got to wrap this up because I'm starting to receive messages from another client," she said as she returned to our conversation.

"Well, jeez. Where do I begin here? Does he miss me in this life? Won't he be lost without me?" I cried, clutching a Sara Lee frozen buttermilk doughnut to my breast.

"His feelings of loss for you are so great that he has become impotent. Many nights he just roams the streets looking for women who resemble you. He is beside himself," she answered while making strange nasal sounds. Like she was taking a hit off a joint or pulling on a pair of tight pants. "Ah, hang on . . . this is the last piece of information I will be receiving because it's starting to grow faint . . . ah, yes . . . you should go and wait for him near the strip joint at Forty-second and Eighth Avenue . . . and wear a rain coat," she said signing off.

Imagine that . . . he misses me desperately. And here

I thought all this time he had purged me from his memory bank. I will have to call Evie and tell her the good news.

JUNIE: Evie, I have fabulous news. He's desperate without me.

EVIE: How do you know this? Did he call you?

JUNIE: Ah, no . . . but almost. Alana, the psychic from Brooklyn, told me that he walks the streets in search of women who remind him of me.

EVIE: So what? He's picking up prostitutes that look like you and you consider that good news? Doesn't that make you nervous?

JUNIE: God no. He can't sleep at night because of the intensity of his feelings. He just can't cope with his feelings, that's all. But she says he's coming back . . .

EVIE: I got news for you. Alana, your psychic from Brooklyn, is fucking with your head, honey. Sol and I ran into him, he was with Mora Tempelton at the Jockey Club last Thursday night and he looked desperate all right, *desperate to get laid by Mora Tempelton, who was lookin' pretty desperate to get laid by him too.*

JUNIE: (What a bitch, that Evie.) You saw him out with Mora Tempelton?

EVIE: Yep.

JUNIE: (Just go ahead and say it: I'm the mother of all suckers.) He's . . . happy then, I take it?

EVIE: Honey . . . he was bordering on the ecstatic.

JUNIE: (I am never leaving my apartment again.) Well . . . then I'm [pause to hyperventilate] truly happy for all of his newfound joy.

EVIE: Get on with your life, honey. You are floundering in your own bullshit right now. I know that it's terribly painful and you feel as if someone is ripping your heart out of your chest, but you've just got to move on now.

JUNIE: I will . . . just let me sleep on it for one more month.

I am experiencing another mood swing. I didn't think it was humanly possible, but I have reached a brand new Olympic low. I feel as if I've been hit by a tidal wave, a gigantic love tsunami.

It's moments like these that I understand why I don't feed myself. I feel so at sea with my emotions, out of control with no place safe to feel anything except underneath my own tear-stained sheets. The only reason I called Alana was to get some hope, some promise that my future would get better. Because right now, as I speak to you buried beneath my fluffy white comforter, I am in the dumper. As Evie correctly pointed out, Alana isn't going to change my life, only I can do that. And the looming question is, How am I going to build a happier life for myself? "Pick your ass up out of that bed, clean up your apartment and go make yourself something to eat. You are going to have to practice what you preach now, Junie," Evie said before hanging up.

But I like being a hypocrite.

Now I understand why I don't want to cook for myself. It feels like an enormous scary leap into a black hole. I always pray that my faith in myself will kick into gear before I have to take any action. But it never works like that, does it? You have to take the action to get the faith. And that is what a clever cook remembers. She cooks herself one hot meal as an act of faith. It's something tangible I can do while I'm trying to pull myself out of this black void. The transition between having no self and planting the seed to a self feels as terrifying as jumping off a cliff, because it means letting go of everything that I think and feel about myself and doing things that feel foreign and strange. It is like I am a stranger in my own mind and body. A sense of self and feeling of dignity are the outgrowths of a woman who has consistently fed herself—physically and spiritually. The hardest thing I ever did was to finally pick my ass up out of my bed. It was the first act of faith I ever took for my own life.

So I got up out of bed, brushed my hair and went to the store for the ingredients for Dijon-lemon chicken. As I stood at the meat counter, figuring out what I needed for the recipe, the butcher yelled across the freezer case, "Whaddayawant?" I sheepishly answered, "I would like one chicken breast, please." Well, he looked at me as if I had asked him if I could have sex with a Smithfield ham. "You want me to go to all this trouble for one lousy chicken breast?" he growled, wrapping up my tiny breast. "What's wrong with ya? Can'tcha' get a boyfriend to take ya out?" Without flinching, I picked up my solitary breast, carefully placed it in my shopping basket, looked right back up at him and said, "GO FUCK YOURSELF."

Okay, so I won't be dining at the Junior League House of Greater New York any time soon. Granted, my reaction was a little crude. What I need is to keep the focus on my life and not on my dismal past. As I stood in my kitchen making my dinner I kept thinking to myself, Let go now, Junie, just let go. Tears ran down my face as I unwrapped my baby breast. *I am never going to throw myself away again, never.* I repeated this sentence as I chopped some garlic and threw it in the skillet. I burned the garlic because I forgot to pour some olive oil into the pan, but so what. I am in the midst of digging deep inside of myself and finding those parts of me that I have tried to suffocate with junk food and casual sex. I can't stop crying. I feel as if a poison is being drained out of me, the poison of self-denial, of self-hatred. I always thought it was other people who abandoned me, but I abandoned myself. Who would ever think a lousy pan of Dijon-lemon chicken would be responsible for a spiritual breakthrough? I am *finally* present within the circumstances of my own life and what a rude awakening it is. I'd give anything to be one of those dopey sluts on those beer ads right now.

I called Sharon and screamed into her answering machine to let her know I was back on the road to recovery. Before she got on the plane back to Dallas, she said one last thing: "I know that until I've heard you scream you'll just continue to destroy yourself with men who don't give a rat's ass about what's inside you."

I ate my Dijon-lemon chicken in the hallway because that is where I am emotionally—standing in a hallway. I got a place mat and a candle and sat down to eat my dinner on the floor of my hallway. Chewing ever so slowly while tearfully staring at my cherry red toenails in the candlelight. I was afraid I might choke to death if I swallowed the warm lemony breast. Shouldn't I be listening to a Helen Reddy album as I did this? I mean, I'm becoming a woman at this very moment, aren't I?

To bury myself in food is a way I try to control my pain. To stuff myself is to wed the physical loss with the emotional suffering. It's my attempt to seal up my bottomless pit. The problem with therapy and self-help books is that the suffering remains as a constant circling of intellectual warfare. Words cannot penetrate my sorrow. Truth—if there really is any in a relationship—is beyond my reach at the moment. But I have fed myself; that much I know. I have fed myself.

As I sit in my hallway, I twirl a buttered noodle with my fork. I feel a dizzy sense of comfort and peace within all of this shifting of emotions. It's an edible prayer signaling me a different end to this relationship. I am feeding that place between my heart and stomach, and things don't feel as confusing as they once did. I gave him my spirit and I am in the process of getting it back. No longer do I feel as haunted by the emptiness inside of me, that cold clang in my guts . . .

As I surf between waves of hope, anger and self-pity I see that there is nothing more to think about. Nothing makes sense when you try to have a spiritual understanding about love. To tell you the truth, I don't want to miss the stupid prick anymore—it's too exhausting. And another thing—it's too damned lonely to hang out on the spiritual plane of love all by myself. The only people out there like that are Kafka, Janis Ian, van Gogh, Billie Holiday, Marilyn Monroe, Dr. Joyce Brothers, Frances Farmer, Goethe, Mary Tyler Moore, Paramahansa Yogananda, Lou Reed, and the Duke of Windsor and his American-born wife What's-her-name. The weird thing is you don't even have to be dead to go out on the love plane; it's like Club Med—they'll take anybody. No suitcase, no drugs, no tanning lotion—all you need is a broken heart.

I've booked enough miles on this 747. It's time to disco.

I'm going to call my girlfriend Karen to come over and watch the Home Shopping Club with me. It's sort of a ritual we have when things are shitty in our lives—we shop via satellite. She is the only friend I have who will wholeheartedly hate anybody who I hate. It doesn't matter if she knows them or not. If I hate 'em, she hates 'em. I just love that about her.

Karen was on the cover of *Self* and *Mirabella* this month. It's odd, but it always takes me a few minutes to figure out if it's her or not. The expression she is wearing is never her own. They've got her wearing that every-woman-jumps-around-with-a-fuchsia-colored-scarf look. You know, like those panty shield ads. In person, her eyes are usually furrowed down as she chews on her bottom lip as she's reading an architecture book. I've never seen her with that silly pout she does for the camera. In fact, I have never seen any woman do that kissy-faced you-kicked-me-first sort of pout in person. Why do they always have models give that look in pictures? I'll have to ask her.

It's always a high point in my month when I receive my magazines and see Karen done up like a drag queen. They've got her looking very androgynous this month. I wonder if that black leather dog collar is really choking her or if they have just styled her to look like she is choking. I'll have to ask her.

I don't think she enjoys her beauty now the way she did in her twenties. She has grown tired of always having to prove to the world that she is not stupid, not vain, not conceited and not put on this earth to seduce everyone she meets. Karen looks like Sophia Loren's second cousin, with big, full Italian lips, wall-to-wall cheekbones and green eyes that are small and mysterious. Karen is convinced she is fat, but she is *definitely* not fat. She has full breasts and hips which she has confused as fat. This incessant confusion about what her body looks like keeps her in search of the perfect diet aide. I am her flock of one. We always buy useless diet shit together—pills, elixirs, whole-grain potions, diuretics, fat-free treats. . . . We would be very rich women if we didn't spend all of our money on useless diet shit. P.S.: We never use any of it, we just buy it. It gives us hope that someday we'll be in control of our bodies. When you meet her in person, her long curly hair always hangs in her face. She's been sort of trapped while in the middle of a relationship. This has made her very serious lately.

"The swimsuit clients that have booked me since I was eighteen sent me home last week because I couldn't fit into their stuff," Karen said, dumping her backpack down on my living-room floor.

I'm glad that I called Karen tonight. She's the only person I want to see right now. Karen's depressed and I find it very comforting to know that I do not have to get out of my flannel jammies and pretend to be happy. I have a low tolerance for other people's joy these days. I still derive great pleasure from other people's inner torture, so don't think all this enormous change is going to make me into a sweet, adoring woman with soap bubbles floating out of my mouth. That would take more than an emotional transformation—it would take a brain transplant. I am still the same vulgar, ruthless bitch I was in chapter 1, with a little more wisdom and compassion. Plus, if you must know, I've put on some weight because I have gone into the second stage of an emotional separation. No longer am I anxious and strung out with anger and rage. Now I am into babying myself. I'm nesting, feeding myself and letting people I really trust back into my life.

Jesus, even my feet look pudgy.

"You look no different than you did three years ago," I told Karen. "Their suits have just gotten so goddamn skimpy. I've seen more cloth on a piece of lint."

"Nope. They're not going to use me anymore because I'm out of shape and too old to be prancing around in dinky bikinis. When I called my booker, I asked her point blank, 'Am I too old or too fat?' " she said kicking off her cowboy boots.

"What did she say?"

"She said I was both. . . . I hate my life."

Karen kicked her legs up onto the bed as she flipped through channels with the remote. She spent her twenties jumping from country to country on different modeling assignments. She doesn't have the personality of a beautiful woman: She's not gregarious, doesn't really like to go out much at night and has an almost sisterly relationship with most men. "I was a fat, ugly girl for so long that I had become the friend of the girl guys wanted to be with. The first guy I ever slept with was with me because he wanted my best friend Theresa. I guess he got drunk enough that he couldn't tell the difference. He called me the next morning to tell me not to say anything to her about what had gone on between us—it might upset her. I'll never forget how that felt," she said, cracking open a diet ginger ale.

I always grew up with the understanding that if you were beautiful, you were loved. I guess that's not true. Before I met Karen I thought all beautiful women were just automatically loved. I guess that's why everybody hates beautiful women. I never think their suffering is real or lasts very long. Beautiful women always have those vain, snotty looks on their faces in magazines. And when you see them in person, they don't look anyone in the eye. Their glance just sort of drifts over your head. They look like they don't need anybody because they've got everybody. Karen reminds me that for all of her beauty and success she still has to fight for her own dignity. "My beauty has never brought me love, Junie. Sex, yes; it has brought me lots of sex, but not love."

Karen moved to New York by herself when she was eighteen. In the beginning she modeled fur coats down in the garment district for fifty bucks a day. She moved from fur shows to shoe shows to ladies foundation shows until she learned how to lock in store buyers at a glance. With a steady hand and a brown pencil she could fan out her eyebrows into a narrow point. It helped to make her face softer, less crow-like and sharp around the eyes. Using the same brown pencil she could draw her lips with a slightly fuller kiss. Karen learned how to arch the collar of a shirt to spotlight her face and hair. As she walked down the runway she worked two distinct fashion looks. For the male buyers, she would twirl lightly in front of them, and tip her head down while casting her eyes upward, staying right below their eye level. She'd hold them in a trance while she wet her lips and steadied her gaze, making sure not to interrupt the seduction, then she'd whirl around one more time, never losing eye contact for a second, and posed until the next model began her twirl. For the female buyers, Karen would not twirl but would pose with her right knee bent slightly to the right. Then she would tilt her head up with her eyes baring down on the tops of their heads. She would mirror their expressions. If their eyebrows jutted up above their brow bones, so did hers. If they sat expressionless, so was she. Whatever their reaction, she would reflect it without ever breaking eye contact. Just like a mime. Her posture was more erect and dominant with the women seated in the front row. She would turn once again, pull her head up a little higher this time, give a slow, steady smile and drift down the runway. Modeling had taught Karen how to become any woman she wanted to be—confident, knowing and magical—for a moment.

She started to get print work because photographers knew she could work whatever look they wanted—the foreign bitch sipping a cappuccino in a café in Paris, the dizzy secretary bouncing around file cabinets in black polka-dot tights, the lonely maiden in the shower wrapped in a green velour towel. She could turn herself into a thousand different women in one afternoon. Her work, however, has taken an enormous toll on her self-esteem. At age thirty-six she often feels over the hill.

Karen shares an apartment with her boyfriend, Steve, who works as an environmental engineer. Their apartment has been under construction for the past two years. Steve designed it himself using Karen's money. The rooms are stark white, with white overstuffed canvas couches and chairs. A little cold to the touch, just like Steve. He refuses to finish the kitchen until he finds the perfect Adriatic blue Italian tile for the wall behind the stove. The kitchen remains gray sheet rock with no cabinets, no drawers and no sink—just a four-burner gas stove and a mini refrigerator. Karen washes the dishes in the bathroom sink. I can't remember how she and Steve met. The most important facts about Steve are that he likes sushi, doesn't like tempura, likes beige cashmere turtlenecks but doesn't like Karen to moan during sex—it upsets his concentration.

"I want to get that Ruta Lee Diet Spray, so call me when it comes on. I saw her talking about it on the Home Shopping Club a couple of weeks ago when I was in Toronto. I'm going to take off my makeup." She jumped off the bed. "Another day, another doughnut."

I laugh when I hear her say this because I know she'll get it—it's supposed to be the aerosol essences of chocolate mousse–mint surprise or something. And she'll spritz her mouth with it right after she's wiped out an entire carton of Ben & Jerry's Cookies and Cream. And then she'll wait and pass me the purse-size can of chocolate mist so I can hose my mouth down after I've scraped the bottom of the bowl of mashed potatoes made with cream cheese and butter. Shit, if this stuff works then I should just spray the entire room.

"I love to eat hot rice pudding with tons of butter and brown sugar," she said as she pulled on her Grateful Dead sweatshirt, "*but* I have to eat it alone. I don't want Steve around. It's something I like to do by myself."

"I like to eat popcorn that's dipped in Smuckers caramel sauce, but I have to eat it in a certain way—big sticky handfuls," I said, laughing.

"God, you make it sound so sexual," she said.

"Hey, it's almost as good as oral sex."

"Giving or receiving?" she asked with an arched eyebrow.

"What do you think? Receiving, for Christ's sake," I said, like it happens to me three times a day.

"Well . . . aren't you the lucky one."

"Steve doesn't?" I asked, giving her a sidelong look.

"Never."

"Have you ever asked him?"

"I don't think that's something you have to ask for, if you ask me."

"Can't you lightly suggest?" I asked.

"Nope."

"Then might I interest you in a bowl of caramel-smothered popcorn?" I said, giggling.

"No . . . because you know what I really want? I want a giant bowl of Kellogg's Frosted Flakes swimming in a pool of Hershey's chocolate milk with a bunch of sliced bananas doubling as life vests." She smiled.

"You'd better run down to the store before Ruta hits the channels."

"I think Ruta looks terrific," Karen said, slurping up a spoonful of Frosted Flakes.

"Lifeway Delicious Diet Spray—satisfies your urge to snack and overeat."

"This looks like just the thing we need," Karen said.

"Comes in Mint-Chocolate, Lemon-Lime and Berry Supreme—with a natural appetite suppressant."

"I think I'm going to get the four-pack for thirty-seven fifty. I guess I'll get the Mint-Chocolate, but maybe I should get one can of Berry Supreme too. Which one do you want?" Karen asked as she pulled out her American Express Gold Card.

"Put me down for a four-pack of the Berry Supreme. I don't think I eat enough fruit."

"This is going to be great when I'm starving and I'm starting to get the jitters. I'll just take a couple squirts," she said as she dialed the number.

"Too bad they don't have a purse-size can for suppressing emotional agony and self-torture," I said, staring at the television.

"Yeah."

Karen pointed out to me that since I had just fed myself my first hot meal that I shouldn't be wanting to stuff my face with Smuckers caramel-covered popcorn. "I thought that when you feed yourself, you don't want to eat junk food anymore. Isn't that what you said?"

Well, for Christ's sake go ahead and shoot me. I mean, really, I'm not Lassie. You can't paper train me in one chapter. Karen of all people should know better than to make a statement like that.

"Karen, you try going six months with no sex and tell me it doesn't make you want to eat something sinful and gooey."

But she has a point. I have to start applying some discipline to my eating habits. It's just so hard when I have this flood of emotions churning around inside me. Sinful, gooey food has an important place in my life while I stay camped in this sexual desert. The lack of something creamy, or gooey or downright kinky cuts me off from any feeling of sinful luxury. I long for someone to give me permission to be sensual, and I've got to cut that shit out. I want my own sense of vitality and freedom, damn it, to sow my own wild oats. Cooking helps me channel my eros into something imaginative and sensual. I must kick start my creativity because I'm losing the zing in my life. And a few kernels of caramel-dipped popcorn ain't gonna kill me. I've just got to get more courageous about how I express myself. Maybe I'll develop a new flavor of International House coffee.

When I stuff myself I'm too tired to think—to want more for myself—to have the energy to change. Just like when I starve myself; then I feel sexless and dead, like I'm too jittery and weak to have any rock-solid concentration. I just vibrate with hunger. I've got to feed this zing thing because it's the lifeline out from my goose-down tomb. I'm like a can of paint waiting to make a splash. . . . I can't wait anymore.

"Karen, we've got to channel our tremendous sexuality into something creative. We've got to get cookin'."

Karen and I always talk about sex, but now I want to explore and she's my comrade in the kitchen so she's got to go with me. Lately, Karen's been burying herself in food while she's been on the road. "Hey, Junie, just because I am in a relationship doesn't mean that I am having great sex. Now pass me the Frosted Flakes." She poured herself another bowl. Her life lacks zing too. You've got to be a clever cook not to lose the zing—so damn clever. Karen and I have got to get cookin'.

FOOD THAT REFLECTS A WOMAN'S NEED FOR SENSUALITY

Rice pudding

Macaroni and cheese

Mashed potatoes with butter and sour cream and then more butter

Fettucine Alfredo

Ice Cream—any flavor, any time of day, by the gallon

Marshmallows dipped in peanut butter

Anything with a Velveeta topping

Chocolate pudding—instant, not from scratch—with whipped cream

Oatmeal with butter and brown sugar

Creamed spinach

Raisin scones with butter and jam

Popcorn smothered in caramel sauce

Soggy Frosted Flakes in chocolate milk with sliced bananas

Baby food with Cool Whip

Evie told me once that she finally experienced her own creativity and sensuality when she started to fix herself one hot meal a day. "Christ, even prisoners on death row get a hot meal once a day. I can at least do the same for myself. You know, it was the one thing I could do that called on me to use my intuition. I loved to stay home on Friday nights and play around in my kitchen." I gave Evie recipes for white bean chili with sirloin tips, fettucine with artichoke hearts and walnuts, and spicy Brazilian black beans with rice—very simple things to start.

Instead of the Dijon-lemon chicken, I would go with the Brazilian chicken with black beans and rice for the first time out cooking for yourself at this stage. Had Karen caught me on a better day, say, like tomorrow, I would have invited her over for some delicious Brazilian-style food to eat while we shopped via satellite. What's great about this rice dish is the variety of things you can add to it. Most of the time I add large pimento-stuffed green olives, chopped bell pepper and yellow corn and serve it with an avocado and papaya salad with hot chili dressing. But you can also add chicken, shrimp or pork and even some stewed tomatoes. Whenever you're cooking, keep in mind that if there is an ingredient called for that you don't like, it can always be substituted. It's also important to remember when making any type of rice dish to use chicken or beef broth instead of water because they will give the rice a richer fuller flavor. (If you are a vegetarian, use a vegetable stock.)

While we were viewing the Connie Stevens's Forever Spring line of beauty products on the tube, Karen and I decided to make a list of all the things that excite us.

"Put down 'masturbate.' Go ahead, you first," I said.

"Oh God, I can't. What if someone found this list? Let me start with 'going to the Planetarium and learning about all the planets and stars.' Then I'll put down 'masturbate.' Just let me ease into this."

Junie's List

- BUY A SHEEP DOG
- LEARN to BE A MYSTIC
- DYE MY OWN HAIR
! *!* MASTURBATE *!* *!* !!
- LEARN how to SPELL
- LEARN not to SAY "FUCK" ALL the
                                        time
- READ the NATIONAL EQUIRER
- EAT, BUT not STUFF

Karen's List

① LEARN how to PAINT.
② BUY A Mountain BIKE
③ LEARN to LIKE Fruit.
④ LEARN to LIKE men
    who AREN'T PERVERTS!
⑤ LEARN to not hate
    MY FAT ASS
⑥ M.A.S.T.U.R.B.A.T.E.
⑦ Registar to vote, then
    masturbate some
    more.
⑧ EAT, BUT not STARVE

Bye

"That's all I can think of for the moment. Just promise me we can still shop for useless shit, like lavender mascara. We can still get stuff like that, right?" she asked, while eyeing the Connie Stevens's Loofa Algae bar for $7.00.

"Absolutely," I answered as I watched Connie hawk her beauty products.

"You know what I want to make? I want to make a big thing of potato leek soup. I always loved that as a child. Do you have a recipe for that? Connie Stevens looks really great, don'tcha think?" She pulled out her American Express card again.

"Yeah, she really does. It's like none of these broads from the sixties ever gets old—they just get blonder. I'll dig up that recipe for you in a minute," I answered while turning up the volume with the remote.

"Well, then I'll want to make that. All I have been eating for the past few months is shit. I've got a lot of changes I got to make in my life, Junie, and I've been avoiding them. That's why I've been stuffing and starving myself. I'm scared I'm gonna wind up a bag woman."

"Why do you think you'll wind up a bag woman when you have been one of the most successful models in the business? I mean, God, you got yourself this far. You'll figure out something."

"I think I should talk to Evie about how I should go about changing my career. She's always great at mapping out a plan of action. And I have got to do something about Steve."

"Are you and Steve having problems?"

"No, not really . . . well . . . yes. I mean, we're not fighting, but we're not close. I don't think he understands how hard it is for me to still be modeling. He thinks it's this stupid job that pays all this money. I never tell him about when a client cancels me, or when my booker tells me it's time to move to something else because I'm getting too old for the business. What am I going to move on to? Where am I going to go? I have no college education, no real skills . . . all I do is jump on airplanes. I think that's why I've been holing up in hotel rooms stuffing my brains out. No one can fix this but me, and I don't know where to start. This is so goddamn sick—to feel worn out at thirty-six. I thought by now I'd be married with a couple of kids. I never planned on being a working woman. I never set up my work to be a career. I thought of it as a temporary job until I got married. Everything feels like it is out of control."

What am I supposed to say to her? "Gee, Karen, don't worry. We can spend thousands of dollars on plastic surgery. And piss all our money away trying to look like an adolescent version of our older selves. And marry men who love us for our breast implants." Life is so goddamn humbling when you've assumed somebody else will be there to give it meaning. I understand what she's saying. To keep myself isolated, longing for some guy who doesn't give a shit about me, keeps me walled off from any real change. (Some truths in life are easy to know but hard to apply. This feels like one of those truths.) We've got to get cookin' . . .

"So, look, we're going to get some zing and learn some new tricks. Then maybe life won't feel so small. Maybe Evie will know of a job you would like to do," I said.

Karen wiped her tear-filled eyes on my pillowcase. "Who's gonna have a job for a fat, over-age model with no college education?"

"Karen, you are not fat. You are not over-age. And you are not unemployable. But you are not gonna feel better about yourself until you give yourself a chance to just live as a normal woman. None of this superwoman shit. We have to be very determined about this because we are two nice broads who are sensual and creative and clever . . . yeah, really clever. Nothing's gonna change with us sitting in here watching the Home Shopping Club."

"And what makes you think we're so clever?"

"We are clever enough to know we need something in our lives that makes us feel happy and alive. And we are clever enough to know how to feed ourselves and we are clever enough to know . . ." I said as I picked up her American Express card.

"To know what?"

"To know where to buy a couple of great vibrators."

Life is hard.
Change is slow.
Hope is all I got.
—JUNIE

Karen's Rice Pudding

SERVES 4

1½ cups milk
5 tablespoons white sugar
1 tablespoon melted
    butter
2 teaspoons vanilla
2 teaspoons almond
    extract
5 eggs, lightly beaten

½ cup raisins soaked in
    ¼ cup hot water for
    2 to 3 minutes
2 cups cooked long-grain
    rice
1 teaspoon lemon juice
1 tablespoon brown sugar
1 teaspoon cinnamon

Preheat the oven to 325 degrees. In a large mixing bowl combine the milk, white sugar, butter, vanilla, almond extract and eggs using a wire whisk.

Drain the raisins and dry with a paper towel. Add the raisins, rice and lemon juice and pour into a greased 8 × 10-inch baking pan. Bake for 45 to 50 minutes, or until toothpick inserted into the center of the pudding comes out clean. Sprinkle with the brown sugar and cinnamon and set the pan under broiler about 3 inches from the flame for 2 to 3 minutes, or until topping bubbles and turns a dark golden brown. Serve hot or cold.

Dijon-Lemon Chicken with Capers

SERVES 2

1 tablespoon butter
½ yellow onion, finely
    chopped
1 clove garlic, minced
½ cup chicken broth
½ cup lemon juice
2 tablespoons Dijon
    mustard

1 tablespoon capers,
    drained
¼ cup white wine
    (optional)
2 boneless chicken breasts
Salt and pepper to taste

In a large skillet on medium heat, melt the butter, add the garlic and onions, and sauté until the onion is translucent. Add the chicken broth, lemon juice, mustard, capers and white wine and stir using a wire whisk.

Add the chicken to the sauce. (If you're watching your weight, remove the skin after cooking; this will help keep the meat moist.) Cover skillet with lid and simmer on medium-low heat for 20 to 25 minutes, or until there is no pinkish cast to the chicken, turning the breasts at least once. The sauce will reduce and thicken into a thin gravy-like consistency.

Serve over rice or noodles.

Fettucine with Artichoke Hearts and Walnuts

SERVES 4

½ pound of fettucine
4 tablespoons olive oil
½ cup walnut halves
1 14-ounce jar artichoke
    hearts

½ cup grated Parmesan
    cheese
2 tablespoons basil

Pour 3 quarts of water into a large stock pot and cook pasta according to package instructions. Drain and place it back into the pot. Place the pot on a low flame and add olive oil, walnuts, artichoke hearts, Parmesan cheese and basil and toss to combine. Serve warm.

Note: It's cheap, it's easy. . . . You'll grow to love this recipe more than your own children.

Brazilian Chicken and Black Beans and Rice

SERVES 4 TO 5

1 8-ounce package
    chicken-flavored
    Mexican-style rice
    (see Note)
1 16-ounce can black
    beans, rinsed and
    drained
1 cup corn, canned or
    frozen
1 bunch scallions,
    chopped
½ cup pitted black olives,
    sliced lengthwise

4 cups cooked, diced
    chicken meat or ½
    roasting chicken
½ bunch fresh cilantro,
    chopped
1 ripe avocado, sliced
1 12-ounce jar good
    quality salsa
1 cup sour cream
1 large bag tortilla chips

Prepare the rice according to package instructions. Add the black beans, corn, scallions, olives, chicken and cilantro into the rice and toss to combine. Transfer to a platter. Garnish with the avocado slices, salsa, sour cream and tortilla chips.

This salad should be served cold, but hot's okay too.

Note: Look for Vigo brand or other Mexican-style rice in the Spanish or Mexican food section of your grocery store. You can also add 1 package of chili seasonings to water prior to boiling regular white rice.

White Bean Chili with Sirloin Tips

SERVES 3 TO 4

1 pound sirloin tips, cut
    into ½-inch cubes
1 large yellow onion,
    chopped
2 cloves garlic, minced
2 tablespoons olive oil
½ cup red wine
1 bay leaf
1 16-ounce can crushed
    tomatoes
1 4-ounce can tomato
    paste

1 tablespoon ground
    cumin
1½ teaspoons crushed red
    pepper flakes
1 teaspoon sugar
1 tablespoon hot sauce
1 16-ounce can white
    beans, rinsed and
    drained
Fresh chopped parsley
    and cilantro for
    garnish

In a large stock pot, brown the meat with the onion and
garlic in the olive oil until the onions are translucent. Add
the wine, bay leaf, tomatoes, tomato paste, cumin, red
pepper flakes, sugar and hot sauce. Bring the mixture to
a rapid boil, reduce the heat and continue to cook for
another 30 minutes, or until meat is tender, stirring occasionally to keep meat from sticking to the pan. Add the
white beans, then transfer to serving bowls. Garnish with
the parsley and cilantro and serve hot.

Curried Winter White Potato Leek Soup

SERVES 6

3 slices of bacon, diced

3 medium leeks, trimmed of roots and dark green stems, sliced and thoroughly washed (see Note)

2 medium Russet or Idaho potatoes, cut into ½-inch cubes

1 bay leaf

1 red bell pepper, diced

1 stalk celery, diced

5 tablespoons flour

5 cups chicken stock

2 teaspoons hot curry powder

2 cloves garlic, minced

2 cups light cream or whole milk

Salt and pepper to taste

Sauté the diced bacon in a large stock pot. Add the leeks, potatoes, bay leaf, celery, bell pepper, garlic and sauté fyor 10 to 15 minutes. Sprinkle the flour and curry powder into the mixture and blend well. Add the chicken stock and simmer for 30 minutes, or until potatoes are tender. Add the cream, salt and pepper to taste.

This soup may be served chunky-style or pureed in a food processor or blender. If it gets too thick and starchy, add milk until it reaches the desired consistency.

Note: When cleaning leeks, it is best to soak them in salted water to leech all the nasty, sandy grit for about 5 minutes.

Hi Everybody:

Junie and I decided that you guys needed to know about the fabulous WONDER BRA. This is the greatest push up bra ever made. It's called the poor girl's boob job. I'm telling ya — — Get THIS BRA !!!!! It makes your boobs look huge. Junie + I give them to each other for our birthday. If you ask me, you should get this bra before you plunk down any hard earned cash for, let's say, a microwave oven or blender. This bra is the greatest. You won't be sorry!

Hope we meet someday!

♡ Karen ♡

Back from the Dead

*J*esus, have I gotten fat.

But wait—the news gets worse.

Karen called to tell me we spent $487.92 watching the Home Shopping Club. Not only did we get the Ruta Lee Diet Spray in the four-pack kits in all three flavors, but we wound up springing for Connie Stevens's Forever Spring Beauty and Bath Collection—two separate kits, $129.00 a kit. Plus the blue enamel Royal Egyptian three-piece matching fashion set of drop earrings, pharaoh-style choker/necklace and matching slave bracelet—$27.25. Plus Karen got a Sound design car stereo with cassette player even though she sold her white Rabbit convertible last summer—the price was too damned good to pass up.

But wait—the news gets worse.

My Visa bill came in at $1,637.08, with a late fee of $15.00. From the Lord & Taylor catalog I got the "poured on gold" fitted bodysuit, American-made, in nylon-spandex—$45.00; a luxurious satin-finished quilted robe, ballet length, in polyester charmeuse—$95.00—plus matching gown—$40.00. From Lalique of France, a full lead crystal rendering of the statuette titled "Kitten with Paw Up"—a collector's piece I'm assuming—standing six inches high for $525.00. From the Williams Sonoma catalog, an ostrich feather duster made from farm-raised ostriches that they swear they don't hurt—maybe terrorize them a bit while they're yanking out their feathers—for $27.50. From the Floral Bouquet section of the Oscar de la Renta Collection, I got the black lace nylon-Lycra lingerie set: underwire lace bra with removable straps, 34B—$36.00; thong-style lace panties—$26.00; and lace-satin-Lycra garter belt—$26.00. And let's not forget, Alana, the psychic from Brooklyn, whose pearls of wisdom cost me $187.60. Oh, and one last item—a Chinese dinner for six from Fuk Yew Too for $149.77 plus tip. Depression is a very expensive hobby.

And yes, Karen and I got two wand-style, latex, shock-proof, steel-reinforced electric vibrators for $128.62, shipping and handling included. Which, by the way, is *really* good news.

And now for the totally bad news.

Sharon called and asked if she could stay with me for two weeks while she continues to survey Roland's base of operation. Remember him? The circumcized Republican she met at the Anthony Robbins seminar in Hawaii? Sharon left a message on my answering machine while Karen and I were getting ready for a small dinner party. When we heard her voice twittering on the tape we stopped what we were doing and stared at each other.

"Are you going to let her stay?" Karen asked as she removed all the Chinese take-out boxes from my refrigerator.

"I have to . . . I have absolutely no choice but to let her stay."

"Why doesn't she just stay with him? Aren't they sleeping together by now?"

"Nope. Sharon won't lay this golden goose until there's enough hay in her coop, so to speak."

"Now, wait a minute. Didn't she spend eleven days with him in Hawaii and four more days with him in New York?"

"Yep, and he has spent every other weekend with her for the past six months. He stays at the Dallas Hilton while he's visiting her."

"No blow jobs . . . no hand jobs . . . no nothing? Hey, wait a minute—how does she know he's circumcised?"

As Karen chopped the tomatoes for her bruschetta, she demanded an explanation to the burning question: Had Sharon seen Roland's penis? Frankly, I was at a loss for words. Sharon was always very cagey about her sex life. Back in our college days, Sharon slept with everybody: Hank the pool cleaner, Buzz the aspiring tennis pro, Rob the law student, who later dropped out of college to become a Hari Krishna—a real nice guy, I ran into him at O'Hare Airport once. Yet unlike most women, she never discusses her sex life in detail. Sharon always left me with the impression that she was the Ethel Merman of oral sex. "It's unbelievable what you can learn at a Junior League meeting," she confided when she told me about her honeymoon with Sammy Lovit. (One of the unfortunate remembrances of my youth was that I was booted out of the Junior League for pilfering a bottle of Jack Daniels from Lois Altrump's mother's tennis bag.

Judging from the level of Mrs. Altrump's response, it seems I borrowed the wrong bottle of Listerine, so to speak.

"Look, *you* ask her when she comes into town," I said while I sautéed the onions for the corn chowder.

"Don't you worry . . . I will."

Karen and I have gotten too clever for our own good. Ever since we took a blood oath, we have been cooking together. And let me tell ya, two clever cooks in a kitchen can be lethal—or if nothing else, extremely fattening. But I also have to tell you I am a very happy woman. Yes, I can honestly say that I spend most of my days fat and broke, but happy. (I am sure you want to know how fat I have gotten. Let me explain it this way: If I were a chicken, I'd have grown from being a puny rock Cornish game hen into a roasting chicken who could be mistaken for a capon when I take my clothes off—about a ten pound spread. You must realize this is a very big moment for someone like me, who has never been happy—ever. I always thought happiness was for other people, like people on *Entertainment Tonight*. (Secretly, I have always felt that Mary Hart was too happy. No one should be that happy all the time. Watching her on the tube makes me feel like a failure as a dyed blonde. I also have my suspicions about Leeza Gibbons—again, a bit too happy to be trusted. The jury is still out on John Tesh. While I feel he has suffered, I think he's made a lot of money from it, so it makes him very happy. I get caught in sort of a vicious circle with him.)

You know, I ran into HIM, Mr. nameless, headless torso from the Polaroids, the other day while I was getting out of a cab in front of Lincoln Center. There he was in his navy blue cashmere overcoat carrying a brown leather briefcase. The sun was in his eyes and he squinted like an old man 'til he could see if it was me. "Junie? Hi, Junie. I tried calling you the other night, but you weren't home." He leaned down to kiss me anxiously on the right cheek. I could smell his spicy clean after-shave as he leaned down to kiss me. The scent made me think of the times when we were in bed together toward the end of the relationship. I remember sticking my face in his pillow and smelling that spicy clean after-shave—like a lemon pricked with baby cloves. In the beginning I got high on him. To touch him, so warm and smooth. We'd never sleep; instead we'd play little games together. Like "Junie, the whore from Wisconsin," who would dress up in a lush, red net bodysuit and have bright red lips and fingernails. I'd tell him it would cost him fifteen hundred bucks to have sex with me. He'd put the cash on the nightstand and the business of forgetting would unfold: He'd forget about the stock market that day and I would forget about me. It was fun for a while, but then I'd forget to get up in the morning. And he'd forget to talk to me. Then I'd forget to be on time for the eight o'clock dinner reservation and he'd forget that I didn't come from Wisconsin. As I remembered all this I'd forgotten how depressed I used to be.

He told me his sister had died a couple of months ago when she was struck by a cab while she was crossing Sixty-third and Park. She died instantly. Tears ran down his cheeks and he turned away from the cold, biting wind. "We hadn't spoken in about three months because she was furious at me for not remembering her son's birthday," he said as he removed his gloves to wipe away the tears. Here I thought he was out every night having sex with another shade of blonde hair. The reality was that he spent most of his nights with his mother and brother-in-law taking care of her kids. We sat on the dry, cold cement steps and watched a group of German tourists take a picture of us. "I'm sorry, Junie. I'm so sorry if I caused you any pain. You're a sweet girl—well, maybe not sweet, but . . . you're a good woman." After a while we got up and walked for a few blocks without saying a word. I felt so close to him now that he had finally let me into the part he closed off to the rest of the world. We kissed good-bye in front of an eyeglass store on Columbus Avenue. Had I not played "Junie, the whore from Wisconsin" we could have been great friends.

He had Calvin Klein navy blue needlepoint checked sheets which said they were 100 percent cotton, but I don't believe it. The flimsy thread count drove me nuts. Some nights I'd scratch until I had faint, scaly tracks of dried blood running up and down my arms and legs. If you're not careful, a bad dose of polyester can kill you.

He called me that same night, about two o'clock in the morning and said he was having trouble sleeping lately. He said he didn't like it when Mora spent the entire night with him. He didn't like it when I did either. He stammered on about his sister who was so angry with him the last time they spoke. It was painful to listen to his words so deeply knotted in sorrow. "It waits for you until you're ready," I whispered. "Sadness knows more patience than we do. You think that if you wait long enough it will just go away. But it doesn't. It just sits and waits. . . ." Tears ran down my face. Somewhere in the darkness his voice broke. He cried for a long time. I don't remember what I said, very little if anything. At five-thirty we parted as friends which was something we never were as lovers.

The closeness I had desperately looked for I found somewhere in all the darkness. When I closed my eyes I felt a final release that didn't come from words but from the gentleness that guided the conversation. It was the most intimate moment we ever shared. I doubt we will ever speak again.

(When I give a copy of this book to my mom and dad I am going to have to get an exact-o-blade and cut this page out. They'd positively shit if they knew about Junie, the whore from Wisconsin—just might cut me out of the will altogether.)

Since Karen and I have been cooking, I have been giving to other people without draining myself. There isn't that same hunger for closeness. Now there is something inside of me—warmth. I'm not stuffing and starving to just cope with my problems. I have a life. I have friends. I have a clearer sense of myself. I have ten extra pounds on me that isn't driving me nuts. Who says miracles can't happen? The fact that I am not in perfect shape and don't hate myself or feel like the lowest form of animal on the cosmic food chain is nothing less than a miracle.

The rebirth of another clever cook.

Karen and I decided on a small party—six people. We invited Evie and Sol, who are great dinner guests because Sol will be the bartender and Evie will make her fabulous sesame-mustard salad dressing with honey and soy sauce; it's weird, because of the nutty sweet flavor, but it works. She very cleverly created a fabulous marinade for chicken too. Even though Steve is still on Karen's shit list, we're going to let him come to our party. "You watch, he's going to hate whatever I make," she said as we were making a shopping list. "That's why I never cook for him. If something doesn't look like a picture in a magazine, then he doesn't want to eat it, and I end up thinking I screwed up the recipe."

Karen makes an important point. The whole world of gourmet cooking has blown up into a new religion of gastronomic perfectionism instead of remaining an intuitive art. Clever cooks have been saddled with overcoming the bias against just cooking delicious food. Gourmet cooking has become so high tech it often leaves beginning clever cooks too intimidated to try a recipe using their own intuition.

There are psychological pitfalls involved with cooking today. Let me give you a few examples:

Pitfall #1: People's expectations of what food should taste like stem from childhood experiences. If your boyfriend's Aunt Gaga made the best meat loaf in the world, yours will always be inferior no matter how hard you try.

Pitfall #2: Everyone is always dieting and won't eat your food unless you file a police report listing of all the ingredients. If you're having a dinner party with five or more people, you can rest assured that at least one guest won't eat because you used butter or salt or meat or a bad food combination. But that's not your problem. If they won't eat your food, suggest they go into your kitchen and make something else.

Pitfall #3: Your veal piccata will look nothing like the pretty picture in the magazine, which will convince people that you screwed up. Magazines hire food stylists to make a quarter-pound of beef look like Liz Taylor and are paid a ton of money for their deftness and skill. Take my advice and rip the picture out of the magazine and throw it away. Yours will taste great, and you should be proud of yourself for trying something new.

Pitfall #4: Some people have a very difficult time when someone makes them something to eat. It stirs up traumatic memories of a childhood that was never nurtured with warm, loving food. It is a very painful thing to witness. Sometimes a plate of roasted chicken with rosemary can remind a person of what they didn't have as a child and will render them speechless. Most people like this eat in restaurants because home-cooked food feels too intimate and makes them feel too vulnerable, so don't be upset if they'd rather go to a restaurant. Food can tell a lot about how a person has or hasn't been nurtured. You are a clever cook if you keep this in mind.

Pitfall #5: Life is a bitch, and some recipes just don't turn out. Don't take it personally. Just learn from your mistakes and try to fix them using your imagination. You can usually turn a plate of bad food into something delicious if you add a little imagination. Screwing up a meal is a very important lesson in life. Good cooks, like good people, screw up all of the time.

I explained these pitfalls to Karen as we made the corn chowder together. Karen helped me in formulating Pitfalls #4 and #5. We have become quite the wandering philosophers in the kitchen, and now that I feel better about myself, cooking has become much more fun and relaxing. Karen helps me appreciate the small things in life. Here I am with a wonderful friend, getting ready to have over a group of people that I really care about, and I don't wish I was somewhere else. Until now it has been very hard for me to jump back into life. No, I don't want to go out on a blind date; I'm not ready for that yet. But I am ready to get involved with my friends again. Let me tell you, it is a relief to stand in the kitchen and philosophize about how difficult life can be. What a luxury after so many months of being consumed with my own sadness. I wasn't a very good friend during the past few months, but I think all that time alone has made me a better one. And it is because I have started to use food to care for myself and not to manage my emotions. *Thank you, Jesus!*

All of the preparations for the party were going quite well, except for the house, which was a mess, and me, who looked like shit. Karen ran to the store for me to pick up some white fish and saltine crackers because I was having a culinary breakthrough. The menu lacked a certain pizzazz so I decided, with Karen's approval of course, that we should make something tender on the inside, yet crispy on the outside—Maryland crab cakes. Since crab is very expensive, I decided to cut the recipe with nameless, faceless whitefish, a fish that blends very anonymously with fresh crab.

Most crab cake recipes call for one pound of fresh or frozen crab meat. I used half a pound of fresh crab that I already had and combined it with the whitefish. This is really a very clever trick, especially when served as appetizers at cocktail parties. You get more bang for your buck, and with something as dense and rich as crab cakes, it's very difficult to tell the difference. (Many restaurants will never admit this, but they often use this trick.) To enhance the flavor, I added chopped yellow onion, fresh cilantro, parsley and yellow corn. They are sinfully delicious when served with a red bell pepper–cilantro mayonnaise. Another clever thing to do is to go ahead and fry them up ahead of time and keep them heated in a 200-degree oven, covered with foil until ready to serve. On the gastronomic orgasmatron scale, these crab cakes would be a definite *ten.*

The crab cakes also go very well with corn chowder, Caesar salad, and Evie's fabulous salad dressing on juicy ripe tomatoes and sliced cucumbers. The crab cakes sort of round off the meal as something unexpected. Karen made bruschetta (chopped garlic, tomatoes and basil on top of crusty Italian bread) for the appetizer, which was a damn good idea. Karen and I don't want a lot of hassle with dinner so we prepared everything ahead of time and we had a variety of food for people to enjoy. Our only problem with the menu was Holly—Pitfall #6: a militant, high-fiber, pain in the ass.

Karen's girlfriend Holly is a macrobiotic, dance therapist–rebirth instructor. I didn't know her, but I figured if Karen liked her she would be a terrific person. I was very, very nice to her. Holly, who looks like Sissy Spacek, was absolutely lovely—until she took off her coat. She helped Karen arrange the flowers. She brought along some incense she insisted on burning that smelled like marijuana. I even let Holly meditate on the floor of my bathroom for twenty minutes before the party, though Karen and I both needed to shower and resurrect an evening fashion look.

"What do you mean she's in the bathroom meditating? I've got tomato pulp all over me. I need to take a shower."

"Karen, just go into the kitchen and hose yourself down with some Ivory liquid. She's communing with God in there and I don't want to interfere with her encounter. Just go fix yourself up in the kitchen," I said graciously.

"I wanted to take a nice relaxing bath with some Forever Spring bath pearls. You know, relax a little before everyone arrives," she whined.

"Take a bath when everyone's arriving so you can make an entrance. Let's not get uptight about this."

"Jesus. Just once I'd like to look good in person," she said storming off into the kitchen.

Well, this was the dumbest idea I'd ever had. Holly decided to take a forty-five-minute refuge with the universe, leaving Karen and me to look like we had just walked away from a plane crash. And to make matters worse, when Holly emerged from her transcendental slumber she walked straight into the kitchen and announced, "I thought I should let you both know that I don't eat anything that has a head." Karen pulled her soapy face up from the kitchen sink and grabbed a dish towel to wipe the suds out of her eyes.

"I'm sorry, Holly. You don't eat what? Jesus, this god-damn dishtowel has chopped garlic all over it and now I've got it in my hair," she cursed.

"I don't eat anything that at one time had a head."

"Do you eat anything that has been prepared by someone with a head, or is that forbidden also?" I asked, crouched down to use the refrigerator light to apply my makeup. Karen marched down the hall to go rewash her marinating head in the bathroom. "Holly, I've got bad news for you. Worse than you could ever imagine. Everything in this entire kitchen has been a head of something. I used a head of lettuce for the salad. I used an ear of corn—that was attached to the head of something—for the chowder, I have egg yolks in the dressing and crab heads in my crab cakes." I smiled as I squeezed the blood out of her arm.

Since I have been a clever cook from birth, I accept the fact that I will never make the perfect meal. Maybe back in the fifties, when people were not so self-oriented, a woman could make a meal that wouldn't get any flak. This is no longer the case today. Everybody has strict religious, political and environmental culinary demands that they have incorporated into their social identity. Frankly, I don't give a shit if Holly starves to death at my dinner party. I don't care if she thinks I am a lousy cook. I don't care what she thinks because today's gourmets are destined to fail in someone's eyes. That's why you can never allow other people to judge your talent and skill as a clever cook.

"Do you want to go to a health food store and pick something you can eat?" I inquired while frying up the crab cakes.

"You wouldn't mind? I just don't feel good when I go off my diet. It makes me feel off kilter inside and it goofs me up."

"Well then, I think you should make something you can eat that will make you feel good. Whatever you want to do is fine with me. I want you to feel happy and comfortable, that's the most important thing," I said, patting her on the shoulder.

Go ahead and say it . . . I'm a saint.

Holly returned from the health food store and created a high-fiber growth of some kind made with aduki beans and seaweed and millet. Let's face it, I'd never served a high colonic for a buffet so I'm out of my league here. No, I did not ask her for the recipe, but she made a generous helping to add to our buffet. It didn't go with anything else I had made, but so what? You know, sometimes you have got to live and let live. But if she starts up with any bullshit again about the fact that I accidentally bought colored toilet paper instead of the politically correct hospital white tissue, I am going to throw her aloe vera ass out of here.

Earlier, I had lit handfuls of vanilla scented candles all around my apartment. It was a frosty night and the sweet glow gave the place a very tender and warm feel against the burgundy walls. With the lights turned down low, the room looked very rich and smart, like an English study. A little masculine, but I've got a dark blue couch with a big peacock pattern to give the room a Latin feel and take away the stiffness and formality. I'm neither Latin nor formal, but I'm not wicker and chintz either, although I do have a Laura Ashley dust ruffle on my bed. I guess you could say I am, design-wise, a Spanish wasp.

Steve arrived precisely at seven o'clock wearing a beige cashmere crew neck sweater under a caramel brown suede blazer. He brought a potted Bonsai plant and set it in the center of the dining room table.

"I thought it would make the perfect centerpiece for your table. You could arrange your buffet with small serving plates around it. Because you don't want to use any large, obnoxious serving bowls that will offset the scale of the tree," he said, removing the vase of flowers Holly and Karen had arranged.

I rarely see Steve in person. Our conversations are usually polite and brief as he passes the phone to Karen. I like him in a perverted sort of way. He reminds me of Anthony Perkins in *Psycho*: tall and thin with long stringy fingers and bony knees. There's something obscene about his clean, high cheekbones and tight lips. He always smells like alpine disinfectant—the kind they use to mop up the men's urinals down at the Port Authority bus terminal. I have no idea if he likes me or not. He would never get caught up in the useless dribble of gossip. That would be somehow too personal for him. He remains forever anonymous yet could pick your soul out of a police line-up. He's not someone I'd do drugs with. It's a good thing I gave them up. Knowing me, I'd talk too much.

Steve likes to trim Karen's fingernails before they have sex. Sometimes he brings home pieces of lingerie he's mail-ordered from a special catalog and has sent to him at work. He has a certain type of shoe he likes Karen to wear—cream-colored satin sling backs with velvet ribbon ankle straps that he ties in oversized bows. He tells her to put them on after she has taken a bath with lemon soap. Karen sits naked at the edge of the bed and he ties them onto her ankles. Then he asks her to step into a pair of creamy chiffon tap pants with matching push-up bra. He tells her he likes the shine of the creamy chiffon against her powdered olive skin. Steve remains fully dressed and pulls back the sheets for her to crawl into their bed. The sheets are always crisp white cotton with an eyelet hem. He pulls the white sheet up over her head so you can see nothing but her silhouette encased in soft folds of cotton. He peels off his clothes as he remains hidden from her view. Steve lies naked on top of her and molds his hand over her supple breasts through the sheet. He kisses her warm lips and pushes his tongue down into her, allowing the fabric to rub against the roof of her mouth. Karen removes her bra, but only when he has told her to do so. If she comes out from under the cotton sheet, they have to start at the beginning and do it again until Karen removes her bra without wrestling her head out from under her milky cover. He likes to feel the tip of her high heel scratch against the back of his calf. Steve doesn't mind if he sees her feet. In fact he loves it. Especially when he sees the velvet bows pulled tautly around her ankles. When he sees the silky bows he can penetrate her with the sheet, but only slightly in the beginning. Then deeper, and the filmy gauze sinks inside her. He is wrapped within her. She loves the tension. He loves the separation. They know each other best during moments like these. Karen loves to feel the beat of his pulse as she lies under a cloud of white. He is hot but never sweaty.

Karen told Evie and me this little story one day at lunch. The waiter almost interrupted to ask if we wanted dessert, but Evie shooed him away with one quick swipe of her right hand. I didn't breathe until Karen finished her story. When she got to the crescendo, Evie and I both looked at each other trying to decide if we were grossed out or turned on. With a guy like Steve you are sort of everything at once. We shook our heads and ordered one slice of coconut cream pie to share and ate it with long silver iced tea spoons.

(You may be wondering why I dropped that little bombshell about Karen and Steve, but I felt we could all stand a little sex about now.)

Steve kept to himself for most of the party. He wasn't thrilled with the menu since he had told Karen to make something he could eat, like steamed vegetables with a bowl of rice, which was all he felt like eating these days. Holly made him some green tea. That was all he had for dinner—three cups of green tea.

Evie spent most of the night on the telephone with a hostile client in Missouri. She and Sol are trying to work some deals together so they can start to put Sol's bankruptcy behind them and build their life together. When Karen finished her shower, Evie asked her to have me come into the bedroom for a moment.

"I've got something to tell you," Evie said in a very serious tone.

"Is everything okay?"

"Yeah, I think so. But I don't want you to tell anyone just yet. I'm pregnant."

Oh my God, Evie's pregnant. It brings tears to my eyes just thinking about it. It has always been her deepest dream, one she had given up over the years. Behind her wall of competency and ambition was a woman wanting to have a child. A terrifying wish to have for a woman who pursued success because motherhood seemed totally beyond her grasp. Evie used to take her brother's children for the weekend, and after they left she would call me and cry into the phone, telling me how she wished she could meet someone that she would feel secure enough to have a baby with. Unfortunately Things don't help you build those qualities. Sol taught her how to love in a different way, simply by giving her time to grow to trust him.

"Why is it when you have given up all hope whatsoever and you have accepted the fact that it is never going to happen, it turns around and happens? I wish someone could explain that to me," she said, laughing with tears in her eyes.

"Evie, aren't you and Sol happy? I mean don't you see this as some incredible miracle?"

"Why? Because I'm thirty-eight or because I was on birth control pills for the last twenty years? My doctor told me four months ago he didn't think it was possible for me to have a child. That's why I'm nervous. I don't want to hex this thing by shooting my mouth off just yet. Don't say anything to Sol either. It makes him nervous and he's nervous enough. He never planned on being a father at fifty-four."

"Do you think you should be working so hard right now?"

"I'm going to start working at home. Sol will be there to work the deals and I can help him. I just hope our financial situation gets better by the time the baby comes. Oh hell, I'll sell my fur coat if it doesn't. I've gathered so much useless crap over the years, I'll just sell it all," she said, zipping up her briefcase.

"I wonder if Versace makes black leather maternity clothes," I laughed.

"Yeah, I'm not going to be wearing him for too much longer. It's sweat pants from here on out. I told Sol to get ready—no more tight skirts or high heels. I told him that for the next nine months I'm going to look like a P.E. teacher."

"Oh Evie, Sol could care less about things like that. He never struck me as that sort of man."

"Don't fool yourself, honey. Men are much more visual than women. They like it when you wear sexy things. Women are different. I think women respond to touch and scent."

"I'm just so happy. I can't even tell you."

"Well I am too, sort of . . . I can't really be happy until I see that this thing is really going to happen, so don't talk to me about it a lot. Oh, and by the way, Sol and I are getting married next weekend down in Atlantic City. It's gonna be just the two of us or I would invite you. We just want to do it alone. I always told my mother

I wanted a huge wedding. But you know, I don't care about that anymore. Sol and I don't have the money to have a big wedding, my mother has been driving me nuts lately, and I know everyone will be happy for me anyway. I want to keep things very simple now. As Sol would say, 'No rah-rah.' "

Karen popped her head through the bedroom door to tell us she had set the food out on the buffet. She didn't step into the bedroom because she sensed that the conversation was private and quietly closed the door behind her. When Evie and I joined the party I could see Karen had put back the vase of flowers in the center of the buffet. I found the potted bonsai on the kitchen counter. Sol was using the tiny branches to hold his cigarette as he mixed himself a dry martini.

The buffet table looked beautiful with flowered ceramic pots brimming over with chowder and crab cakes. Karen stuck a big purple geranium in the center of the Caesar salad. (I prayed to God the flower wasn't poisonous.) The bruschetta added a dash of drama against the pale yellow gold of the chowder. Holly's high-fiber growth was a total hit; by the time I reached the buffet there was hardly any left. I saw Evie and Karen sharing a plate of it while they sat on the couch talking to one another. Sol made himself a sandwich by placing a crabcake on top of the bruschetta and then drowning the mess in the bell pepper–cilantro mayonnaise. He had to lean over his plate on his tippee toes so it wouldn't spill all over the floor. Holly had been kind enough to fold the pink linen napkins and refill the ice bucket. Eventually she ate a small plate of Caesar salad and quickly returned for a second helping. Holly told me she liked the lemony crunch of the lettuce leaves. I felt guilty for having been such a bitch to her that afternoon. She and Steve were looking at a book on German photography. Steve pretended not to notice Karen had removed the bonsai from the center of the table. He seemed intent on boring Holly with how different the Germans and French photographers are. Sol seemed happy by himself as he critiqued the variety of food on the table. I was positive he was going to tell me I should have made a broader selection of entrees. Every buffet should be like a Jewish luau, in his opinion. He almost swallowed his tongue when he discovered we were serving Ruta Lee's chocolate-mint mist for dessert.

"You can't serve that garbage for dessert," he said indignantly.

Setting the purse-size cans on a silver tray I smiled back at him and said, "Sol, this stuff is great. You just spray some in your mouth and you trick your brain into thinking you ate a chocolate cake, but you don't gain any weight."

Sol would not allow me to serve the chocolate-mint mist for dessert, so we made incredible apple tarts sweetened with quick brush strokes of apricot jam. (Remember to always keep a couple of packages of Pepperidge Farm puff pastry in your freezer. They are a little expensive but come in handy for last minute appetizers and desserts. Simply defrost the pastry according to the package instructions and cut the pastry into 2 × 3-inch individual squares. Then core and slice paper thin 2 medium Granny Smith or any sour green apples. To prevent the apples from turning brown, soak them in lemon juice and water after slicing and dry them with paper towels before setting them on the pastry. Fan the slices of green apple on individual pastries. Lightly brush warmed apricot jam on top of the apple slices and bake on a nonstick cookie sheet for 10 to 12 minutes in a preheated 350-degree oven. Serve warm with vanilla ice cream. I am a big believer in Pepperidge Farm pastry products and will hock their products pro-bono because they are a clever cook's best friend.) They were a true show stopper. When Sol walked the silver tray of piping hot puffs of baked apples with a sweet pillow of vanilla ice cream melting down the sides into a creamy pool (this is starting to sound like Karen and Steve's sex scene again, isn't it?) everyone let out a weak gasp. The apples were still firm enough to cut with a fork yet were hot and tender from the apricot glaze. The flaky crust was the perfect nest for the tangy combination of apple and apricot mouthfuls. Even Steve partook in this moment of sin. He silently cut each bite diagonally, in the direction of the fanned apple slices. When he finished he breathed deeply and let out a heavy sigh. Sol ate his like a slice of pizza, catching the vanilla drips with the palm of his hand. Evie and Karen shared one tart by pulling it apart with their fingertips. They were careful not to burn their fingers on the hot, drippy apricot syrup so they cooled off each slippery bite in the puddle of vanilla cream. Holly went the holistic route by separating the glazed apples from the crust. She ate each slice of apple one at a time and then finally, when her reserves were all exhausted, she took the plunge and ate the airy crust that was floating in a pool of melted cream. I flipped my tart over so the crust wouldn't get soggy. This way I could eat the golden brown layers slowly, allowing the ice cream to soften into the glazed apples. It was the perfect slice of eros for an otherwise sexless evening. For all of his pissing and moaning, I did notice Sol jot down the recipe. He ate the last buttery slice while he announced to the room that if it were not for him I would have sent everyone home with a can of Slimfast. Sol's bitching helped me to remember what a resourceful person I am in the kitchen. He was definitely impressed. Sooner or later Sol is going to truly convert to the clever cook philosophy. It is all a matter of time. . . .

At the end of the night Karen came into the kitchen to help me with the dishes. Judging from the leftovers it would seem that the crabcakes and the corn chowder were the most popular items on the menu. As I had expected, the Caesar salad was limp with too much dressing, but Karen and I picked at it while we were cleaning up.

"Evie's gonna have lunch with me on Thursday to talk about work," she said, picking up a lettuce leaf with her fingers.

As I leaned against the sink I ate the last spoonful of Holly's high-fiber growth. "What does she have in mind?"

"I don't know, but I figure we can talk about some ideas. I told her I always wanted to have my own plant store, but not here in New York, someplace quieter. She thinks I can do it with the money I've saved," she said, pouring herself some orange juice.

"Would Steve go with you?"

"Never in a million years," she said, dipping a crouton in the chowder.

"What do you think about that?"

"I think he's been screwing someone else for the past two months and he's waiting for me to bring it up," she answered matter-of-factly.

I had a strange sense something like this was going on. I knew she had something to tell me. I think Steve's Thing has been going on for more than a couple of months. Karen has been slowly devouring herself for months. That's why she's been up here cooking with me. I think she's trying to get enough self-esteem together to leave the kinky prick. (I hate it when anybody hurts my friends. It makes me want to go back a few pages and say more shitty things about him.)

"Who is she?" I asked, slamming the refrigerator door.

"The wife of his client. He thinks I don't know, but I do. I knew the first night he slept with her." She poured the soggy salad dressing down the sink.

"How did you know?"

"I knew it when he touched me."

Steve was standing in the doorway of the kitchen holding Karen's jacket. He just stood there looking at her with ice picks in his eyes. Steve looked just like Anthony Perkins did in *Psycho* right before he made steak tartar out of Janet Leigh—just staring at her with a freaky smirk on his face. Evie was right behind him with a load of dishes in her hands.

"Excuse me, Steve, I want to drop these in the sink so I won't feel so guilty about leaving Junie and Karen with all this mess." She did not know what was going on.

"So, tell me, Steve, do you feel guilty?" Karen announced to everyone standing in the kitchen.

Steve stood in the doorway as he talked to the top of her head. "Karen, don't start anything. You always blow things way out of proportion and I'm not going to discuss this with you here. You are just going to make an ass out of the both of us."

"I want to say good night and thank you both," Evie said, trying to get out of the line of fire. "Karen, I will talk to you tomorrow about lunch. Sol and I will take Holly home with us."

"I'll help you get your coats," I said, leaving the kitchen with Evie.

Karen and Steve remained in the kitchen for about twenty minutes. There was a low steady hiss between them. Evie asked me what was going on and I told her to talk to Karen about it in the morning. Steve left by himself without saying a word. Karen stood in the kitchen by herself crying as she washed the dishes. I said good-night to Evie, Sol and Holly and closed the front door quietly behind them. I sat in the living room and waited for Karen to come out and talk to me. I had the feeling she needed some time by herself.

"I'm moving up to Woodstock and opening a flower shop as soon as possible. I'm gonna sell that fucking apartment that I've always hated and I'm going to get a home with some plants and a yellow dog . . . I can't remember the kind right now," she said, sitting on the floor in a teary daze.

"Karen . . ."

"No. My whole life, men have always wanted to be with someone else when they are with me and I can't take it anymore. I've waited my entire life for someone to love me—just me. I've wanted someone to love me, so I was thin for them. I was kinky for them. I was young and perky for them. But now I want someone to love *just me*. Steve doesn't love me. He doesn't love anything. He created me from his own imagination and I followed everything he ever said. I never, ever wanted to, but I did it and it has totally fucked me up."

"Karen, I think—"

"No, Junie, it doesn't matter what you think, because you have no idea. I've lost my dignity to preserve his. I have no dignity anymore. I've known about this bitch for months. She calls and hangs up when I answer the phone. She invites him to her fucking museum parties when I'm out of town. She's forty-six years old and looks fucking great. She's got everything he's looking for— power, status, money—she's got plenty of money and he hates her husband . . ."

This stuff just kills me, although I know it is a good sign that she's getting angry. *Really angry.* Now she has the opportunity to do something about it besides be depressed. She needs to fall apart so she can build a stronger foundation. It's a good thing when a woman can just fall apart; then she can change. She can't change until she gets angry enough to want to try something different. As long as she stays depressed and buried in food, she will continue to allow food to control her emotions and she will not be able to help herself. Now that Karen has started to feed herself, she's not using food to control her anger, to keep it trapped down inside of her, making her feel powerless and constantly abused. This is a good thing. She is not her own victim.

"Karen, whatever you do, will you just take some time? If you want to stay here with me, then fine, you can stay for as long as you like. But I want you to take your time."

"I've taken enough time. I'm done with taking time. I'm going to stay here tonight and I'm going to go home and pack in the morning and spend the day up in Woodstock looking around."

I made up the hide-a-bed for Karen in my living room. We both just rolled our eyes when we saw the white cotton sheets with eyelet hem. Karen had given them to me for Christmas last year. "He's such a sadist . . . and I loved every minute of it," she said, helping me make up the bed. We didn't sleep the entire night. I sat in the green leather chair and ate soggy Caesar salad while Karen made a list of all the things she needed to do. (This is a terrible thing to admit, but I'm so glad that she is going through this and not me. For so long it had been me digging myself out of some hole. I know exactly how she feels and I don't *ever, ever, ever* want to go back there. I feel faith for the first time—ever. My whole life I have desperately searched for it in people, in jobs and in food, only to find some faith in myself. A tiny sliver of dignity for being a woman, and guess what? I found it—buried deep within me. Now the trick will be not to lose it again.)

"You're gonna be really pissed off for about two weeks," I told her, "and then you're gonna go to bed for about six months and then you're going to get up one day and decide to change your life, and then you're going to want to go back to bed, but you won't, you'll take a twenty minute nap and watch 'Oprah' and then you'll fix yourself something to eat that you have to bite with your teeth again because you're sick of creamy food. You'll crave protein, lots of protein, and things you have to eat with a knife and fork and a plate, and then you'll throw the dishes in the sink and then you'll call all the friends you dumped and then you'll realize how fat you've gotten and then you'll change your life, but only after you've had a pedicure. Trust me, I'm the leading authority on 'When He Leaves.' " All this as I modeled my polyester charmeuse ballet-length bathrobe and matching nightgown from Lord & Taylor's.

"No I won't, I'll be over this in a week," she said, biting into a pretzel.

"No you won't, because if you get over this in a week it means that nothing has changed and you'll wind up with the same person doing the same thing in a different town. You need to fall apart for six to eight months to complete a true romantic exorcism. If you run and jump into something else you'll wind up possessed again by some satanic chainsaw magnate. Sometimes the best thing you can do is just go ahead and fall apart. Because if you fall apart really well, you will start to fall together. I think everybody should just fall apart once in life so they can finally get their shit together," I said, pulling on a pair of sweat socks.

"Oh, and you think you've got your shit together now Junie?"

"No, but I've got my shit together enough to know that I'm not going back to where I came from. From here on out I am takin' my time. I don't know what happened to me over the past eight months, but I'm not that lonely, anxious girl I used to be. I've slowed down and learned how to feed myself physically and emotionally. And so have you, Karen. Don't forget that. I did the Club Med at Agony Beach. I don't ever want to go back there again."

Life is short.
Faith takes action.
There are other Club Meds in the ocean.
—JUNIE

Creamy Cheesy Corn Chowder

SERVES 3 TO 4

2 tablespoons butter
1 yellow onion, chopped
1 red bell pepper, diced
1½ cups diced potatoes
2 tablespoons flour
3 cups chicken stock
1 bay leaf
2 cups fresh or frozen
    corn

1 cup milk
1 teaspoon hot sauce
1 cup grated cheddar
    cheese
2 tablespoons basil, pars-
    ley or cilantro as
    garnish

Melt the butter in a large soup pot and add the onion, bell pepper and potatoes. Sauté until the onions are translucent. Add the flour and stir it into the mixture, then add the chicken stock and bay leaf. Cover and cook over low heat for 15 to 20 minutes, or until the potatoes are tender. Add the corn, milk and hot sauce and continue to simmer. Just before serving, stir in the cheese and serve with your choice of basil, parsley or cilantro as garnish.

The Clever Cook's Crab Cakes

MAKES SIX 3-INCH CRABCAKES

1 egg, beaten

½ pound lump crabmeat
½ pound white fish—sole, haddock or cod
1 tablespoon Dijon mustard
1 tablespoon Old Bay seasoning (see Note)
1 tablespoon minced shallots
¼ cup fresh or frozen corn
1 teaspoon Worcestershire sauce
¾ cup crushed saltines
2 tablespoons chopped cilantro
2 tablespoons butter
2 tablespoons olive oil

Place all the ingredients except butter and olive oil in a mixing bowl and blend thoroughly using fingertips. Form the mixture into round, 3-inch crab cakes. Heat butter and olive oil in a heavy metal skillet and sauté the crab-cakes until golden brown on both sides. Drain them on paper towels and keep them warm on serving plate in a 200-degree oven until ready to serve.

Note: Old Bay seasoning can be purchased at fish markets and gourmet shops. It's *not* essential, but is a great sea-food seasoning.

Bell Pepper–Cilantro Mayonnaise

MAKES 1½ CUPS

1 egg
1 tablespoon lemon juice
1 cup olive oil
*2 tablespoons diced red
    bell pepper*

*2 tablespoons chopped
    cilantro*

Place the egg and lemon juice in a blender or food processor. With the processor running, slowly pour in a steady stream of the olive oil. The mixture will start to emulsify (turn creamy white), but continue until all the oil is used. Add the bell pepper and cilantro and blend for about 3 seconds more. Serve cold.

Junie's Lazy Girl's Caesar Salad Dressing (and Salad!)

MAKES 1½ cups

5 tablespoons lemon juice
1 can anchovy fillets
2 cloves garlic, minced
1 teaspoon Worcestershire
    sauce

1 dash hot sauce
½ cup Parmesan cheese
1 cup olive oil

Pour the lemon juice, anchovies, garlic, Worcestershire sauce, hot sauce and cheese into the workbowl of food processor or blender. Puree until the ingredients are blended, then with the processor still running, slowly pour in the olive oil until the dressing is fully emulsified (turns creamy white). Set aside.

To assemble a Caesar salad, wash 2 heads of Romaine lettuce and spin dry in a salad spinner or pat dry with paper towels. Tear the leaves into bite-size pieces and put in salad bowl. Add croutons and toss in as much Junie's Lazy Girl's Dressing as you prefer. Sprinkle more grated Parmesan cheese on top of salad before serving.

Note: This is an eggless Caesar salad recipe. Raw eggs are too risky due to salmonella problems so I don't use them anymore.

Karen's Famous Bruschetta

MAKES 10 TO 15 slices

1 loaf peasant, sourdough
    or French bread
½ cup olive oil
1 pound fresh plum to-
    matoes, seeded and
    diced

1 bunch fresh basil
    leaves, washed and
    chopped
3 cloves garlic, minced
2 tablespoons white wine
Salt and pepper to taste

Preheat the broiler. Slice the bread into pieces ½-inch thick and brush with the olive oil. Toast under the broiler for 3 to 4 minutes, or until golden brown. Remove from the oven and allow to cool.

In a small mixing bowl, combine the tomatoes, basil, garlic, white wine and remaining olive oil. Add salt and pepper. Heap large spoonfuls on top of toasted bread slices and serve.

The Minute-Made Apple Tart

SERVES 4

1 sheet Pepperidge Farm
    puff pastry
2 sour green apples, cored
    and sliced paper thin
    from top to bottom

½ cup apricot jam

Preheat the oven to 350 degrees. Unwrap the pastry from the package and allow to thaw completely. Roll out onto a well-floured surface and cut into 2 × 3-inch squares. Prick the pastry with a fork and brush with a spoonful of apricot jam. Place the apple slices in a fan-like arrangement on the pastry squares and put them on an ungreased cookie sheet.

Bake for approximately 10 to 12 minutes, or until the apple slices are tender-crunchy. Serve warm with vanilla ice cream.

From the Kitchen of Junie Lake

Definition of "Faux Gourmet":

Faux Gourmet: To be free to live one's life
with dignity.   To feel joy in the daily task
of living.   To feed oneself physically,
emotionally and spiritually.   To be a
sensual, erotic woman who knows better than
to stuff and starve herself in order to
contain her feelings.   To be able to love and
be loved.   To live in peace.   To feed herself
one hot meal a day.   To not have to do it
perfectly.   To have faith in herself.

Part II

The Fine Art of
Balancing
Love and Food

Blindsided

"*H*ow do you know Roland is circumcised, Sharon?"

That's how I greeted her when I opened my door. I decided to employ Evie's form of truth serum—peer pressure.

Sharon now looked like a cross between Connie Chung and Marilyn Quayle. Gone were the Cleopatra-rimmed eyelids with the Grecian goddess crescents of black curls from the dark ages of our college years. Gone were the golden tufts of her Morgan Fairchild honeydew blonde cotton-candy swirl from the days of Sammy Lovit. Gone was the country spun simpleness of her Marie Osmond bangs that fluttered in her eyes from her Anthony Robbins days. The hairdo that stood before me was buffed, bobbed and brunette and fell into a shallow flip at her shoulders. Gone were the three-inch press-on nails that had halted any career opportunity. Gone were the too-tight Diane Von Furstenburg cotton wrap dresses. Gone were the slutty, strapless stilettos from her youth. What stood before me now was a woman in search of a Republican cocktail party.

She looked like the type of woman who'd never leave a lipstick ring on her coffee cup after finishing her chicken salad sandwich on whole wheat toast—hold the crust, please. And let's face it, if she had to choose between buying this cookbook and one of Martha Stewart's cookbooks, she'd get Martha's.

"How dare you ask me a question like that? Roland's penis is my business. Now help me with my bags. I knew I should have stayed with one of my sisters from the Junior League, but I said, 'No, Junie needs me right now. She's depressed again in one of her romantic funks.' " She groaned as she pulled the suitcases off her portable luggage rack.

"I am not depressed anymore. In fact, I feel quite jovial and free. I pierced through the eye of the needle . . . my black hole of Calcutta . . . the raging inferno of my own existential nightmare . . . the endless pit of my quest for God-ordained love," I said, trailing down the hallway.

"You mean you got over the motherfucker and will never date anyone like him again," Sharon said straightening her cherry-red double-breasted blazer.

"When did you start using dirty language?"

"During the divorce when everyone, including my lawyer, started screwing me around. Sammy tried to take the house, the two Cadillac Sevilles, the wrought iron patio furniture, the antique rifle collection. One night he stole all the jewelry he'd given me when he broke into the house while I was at real estate school. He took everything but the yellow pages. Now, I need to unpack. Where can I hang my things?"

"God, what did you do? You never told me he ripped you off like that. Why didn't you tell me?"

"Because, baby girl, that chapter of my life is closed. Now where is your telephone? I have to call Roland and tell him I'm here." She set her Coach handbag on the coffee table.

I knew Sharon had gone through a rough time after the divorce. She moved back to her parents' ranch in Plano during that time, where her father built her a little bungalow off the back patio of the house. Daddy Snorkel loved Sharon more than the stuffed deer heads mounted on his office wall. Daddy Snork, which is what everyone called him, owned a number of successful Cadillac dealerships throughout Texas. Twice he had run for mayor of Dallas on the Republican ticket and lost.

Mrs. Snorkel called me a week before Sharon's thirtieth birthday. "Send her a silly birthday card and get her the pink angora sweater set on page one hundred and sixty-two of the Spiegel catalog, will you, honey? My baby is going through a terrible time. She won't talk to anyone, not even Snorkie." Mrs. Snorkel then confided that Sharon had "let go of a baby in the name of Jesus Christ." My heart sank when she told me this because I knew Sharon didn't believe in abortion. "She had to do it, honey. She can't even take care of herself right now and Daddy Snork and I are too old and tired to raise a baby ourselves. I just want to see a smile back on my little girl's face." She sighed into the receiver.

Sharon virtually stopped eating after her abortion. She went from a size eight to a size four in about three months. All she would eat were greasy fried egg sandwiches on whole wheat toast with Miracle Whip. Sharon almost starved herself to death over the abortion, but I don't think she really cared after a while about losing Sammy. It was a relief to have him gone. She never did get her real estate license. Sharon pretended everything was fine whenever we spoke on the phone; she never told me about the abortion. Her mother did.

Mrs. Snorkel has always reminded me of Arlene Dahl. She would spend two hours every morning putting on false eyelashes and teasing her autumn-red Jacques Darcel wig only to walk around the house wearing her emerald green silk caftan with matching rubber thongs. She never went anywhere that didn't have central air conditioning. Mrs. Snorkel is Sharon's best friend. During college when I would come to visit, we would all sit in Mrs. Snorkel's canopy bed and watch the "PTL Club" on the mega-screen television set. We'd all hold hands and pray that Jim and Tammy would get enough prayer partners to build the Heritage USA Park and Condominium Complex. The Snorkels already owned one condominium and were planning to buy two more for Sharon and her younger brother, Bucky. I loved to sit in Mrs. Snorkel's lavender satin bed and eat barbecue beef sandwiches on a bed tray. Sharon would sit wedged between us, and eat cherry-flavored Jell-O made with fruit cocktail and coconut flakes with her Dr. Pepper with plenty of crushed ice. Sometimes we'd stay up until two or three in the morning and sing-along to Tammy Faye's gospel hymns. Mrs. Snorkel always credits those songs with putting an end to my panic attacks. Daddy Snork always tells people it was when he pulled me off one of the mariachi players at Sharon's wedding and yelled at me to lay off the scotch.

I have always been closer to Mrs. Snorkel than to Sharon, and while Sharon was going through her divorce, I talked to Mrs. Snorkel about twice a week. The Snorkels' life seemed to go from bad to worse with each new conversation. Sharon's divorce was just the beginning of the Snorkels' difficulties. Daddy Snork's car dealerships weren't doing so well. Everybody was buying Hondas;

nobody wanted his gas-hogging Coupe de Villes, which was what Daddy Snork was known for throughout the Lone Star State. This was very hard on Daddy Snork's sense of inner magnificence. He's like the Jack Palance of the auto business—rough and rugged. You never know if he's going to punch you in the face or kiss the palms of your hands. Daddy Snork yelled at everybody but Sharon and her mother. The two of them were like his blessed Madonnas.

A couple of nights before Sharon's wedding Bucky and I busted him tinkling ice cubes with a granite-voiced redhead sipping a pink margarita. They were cradled underneath the antlers at the Red Lantern Steak House and Grill. Daddy Snorkel's ego was in search of a full-breasted audience. Bucky just shook his head and ordered another bourbon and water for each of us. We sat in the corner and unscrewed the light bulb from under the red plastic lamp shade over our heads. We sat in silence watching Daddy rub a chip of ice between the redhead's giggling breasts as she slowly sucked the smoke from a Tarryton 100. His fingers looked yellow and frail against her doughy white breasts. We finished the bowl of mini pretzels shaped like sea stars and slipped out the fire exit next to the stuffed antelope head. Bucky and I played gin rummy with Mrs. Snorkel and Sharon when we got back to the ranch. Daddy didn't get home until after the eleven o'clock news that night due to engine trouble.

In the spring of '86 Mrs. Snorkel found a malignant lump in her right breast. She had to have both of her breasts removed because the prognosis was not good. The cancer had spread into her lymph glands under her arms. She lost her show-girl figure and most of her hair by the end of that summer. Daddy Snork drove her once a week to her chemotherapy appointment in his black Coupe de Ville with red leather seats. He would sit in the waiting room and read *Ladies' Home Journal* while he listened to the buzz of the radiation machine. He didn't bother to flirt with the nurses.

Before his wife's breast cancer Daddy Snork slept in Bucky's old bedroom down the hall. When Mrs. Snorkel got sick he moved back into her room and watched the PTL Club with her. They would hold hands as they prayed to God to heal her cancer. Sharon got her first job as a concierge at the Mansion Hotel. She loved working there. She was responsible for handling all the conventions and seminars that came to the Dallas–Ft. Worth area. After work Sharon would come home and cook meals like roasted chicken with mashed potatoes and sliced tomatoes and eat them with her mother and Daddy Snork out on the patio overlooking the kidney-shaped pool. The Snorkels were relieved to see her eat again. Sharon would read the *Daily Word* to her mother on mornings when she felt nauseous from all the chemotherapy. They never discussed what happened with Heritage Park USA or Jim and Tammy Faye. There never seemed to be a good time to bring it up. God was their only pipeline to hope. Mrs. Snorkel liked to play Tammy Faye's Christmas tapes throughout the house all year-round. At the end of our phone conversations, Mrs. Snorkel would often read the Lord's Prayer aloud before saying good-bye.

If there is ever a woman who had dignity and courage, it is Carolyn Snorkel. She is a very clever woman and a wise one too. I had sent a purple Indian print caftan with tiny mirrored beads sewn on it and a pair of matching purple rubber thongs after her mastectomy. She loved it and told me she was going to wear it after she got her face-lift in the fall. Mama Snorkel always said there were three secrets to a happy marriage: separate bathrooms, the ability to fake it and to love your husband with God's heart instead of your own. Even though the cancer had spread to her lymph glands, as each day passed her eyes seemed to grow more serene. She told me once that she was grateful Sharon caught Sammy screwing around with the Herbalife trainee. God had intervened in the perfect way to spare Sharon any more suffering. After her face-lift, Mrs. Snorkel decided to go off all medication and radiation to study the Christian Science form of healing. She has not been to a doctor in six years. God is alive and working in Mama Snorkel and nobody asks any questions.

Daddy Snork has forever been trying to set me up with Sharon's baby brother Bucky, who lives in Lubbock and manages one of the Cadillac dealerships. Bucky and I made out at one of the barbecues during Sharon's wedding celebration. I mean, I pray to God that it was him. If it wasn't, it was Daddy Snork, and I am really going to rot in hell. I remember passionately kissing some guy on the dance floor near the barbecue pit who was wearing a black cowboy hat and who looked like Kyle Petty. What I remember is waking up in Bucky's bedroom with my Calvin Klein pantyhose dangling from one of his child-hood rodeo trophies. I remember picking my head up from his pillow and seeing a big furry spider parked on the wall behind the bed. It was too terrifying to even respond so I planted my head face down on the pillow and went back to sleep until the mid-afternoon. When I woke up, it hadn't moved an inch from when I saw it before. As I reached for my eyeglasses I studied the hairy predator more intensely. It wasn't a spider. It was one of Mrs. Snorkel's false eyelashes that I had borrowed for the wedding. I guess I stuck it on the wall during my fit of passion with Bucky. I didn't want her to think I was ir-responsible by losing both eyelashes, so I saved one. Bucky came into the room holding a giant glass of Tang in his hand. He sat on the foot of the bed and handed it to me.

Just a minute, please.

(Dear Mother and Dad,
You remember Sharon's wedding. I told you all about it so you don't need to read this chapter. So why don't you just flip through the pages until you get to the index. I did a fabulous job on the index.
Love you both,
Junie
P.S. I have no money. American Express is threatening to beat me up. Just thought you might want to know in case you called and I was in the hospital or something . . . but don't worry.)

Let's just hang loose for a minute until they turn the page. They think I'm still a virgin, so I gotta keep a low profile.

Okay, let's hit the sheets.

"You are something else, Junie. My mama told me to watch out for girls like you," Bucky said as he kissed my forehead.

"So what did I do, Bucky? I mean, did you and I do it?"

"Nah. You threw up before we could do it. Mama asked me to stay with you through the night so you wouldn't fall out of bed and crack your head open. She knew nothin' was gonna happen. But you whispered some nasty things in my ear before you puked your brains out and I'm gonna hold you to your word—just not today." He laughed as he patted my thigh through the covers.

"Does Mama Snorkel know I threw up?" I cried, taking a tiny sip from the glass. (What am I doing in a Dallas Cowboys T-shirt and one sweat sock?)

"Yep, she sure does, and she heard you say all those nasty things to me too." He laughed as he unbuttoned his flannel shirt.

"Bucky? Did I do anything I should be ashamed of?" I felt sick to my stomach.

"Not in front of anyone but me, girl." He smiled and crawled back into bed.

I made Bucky promise never to tell Sharon that I had . . . what? To this day I have no idea what happened with Bucky. I do know that when I arrived at the Snorkel ranch Bucky was a virgin and when I left that was no longer the case. The exact time of his devirginization remains a looming question. He crawled back in bed with me under the strict orders that he had to keep his Levis on and buttoned. He read *Auto Week* aloud until he got to the classifieds. Bucky twirled my hair in his fingers. I felt his pulse bounce up through the mattress. The bed frame creaked as he turned on his side, pressing his nose against my cheek. His hair smelled like Sharon's orange blossom shampoo. He asked me if I would have a panic attack if he took off his jeans. I just looked at him and smiled. When Bucky got lucky we knocked the glass of Tang all over the oatmeal colored wall-to-wall carpeting. I told him he couldn't kiss me until he found the Certs in the pocket of my blue linen blazer. I am a Virgo; we're very anal about this sort of thing. Bucky knew that if he was going to reach the edge of the universe he was going to have to find the Certs before I was hit with another wave of nausea. He found them in a matter of milliseconds and crawled back in the saddle. I kept on thinking of Sharon on her honeymoon in Barbados psychically tuning in to the fact that I was screwing her baby brother. Then I thought of Mama Snorkel down the hall in her bedroom sitting right beneath the giant crucifix over her bed, hearing every ooh and every ahh. I knew that she and God were taking notes. I could never watch the PTL Club with her again. Thank God the show has been canceled.

Bucky was an adorable, big floppy puppy with his paws all over everything. He looked up at me with these Milkbone brown eyes—so grateful. I was happy to help him out. The miracle of the moment was that I didn't choke on the five peppermint Certs I had swallowed. Bucky celebrated his miracle on his own. I was like a dead fish frozen in guilt. He asked me if he could go downstairs and make me some scrambled eggs and Cream of Wheat to help settle my stomach. And then asked me if we could do it again later in the afternoon. I said yes to his first question and a shaky maybe to his second. I had to go confess to Mrs. Snorkel. I had to go and tell her I had been whoring it up with her baby boy. I had to. It was my civic duty. Mama Snorkel met Bucky at his bedroom door. She gave him a kiss on the cheek and told him to run downstairs and stay there until the two of us came down for afternoon tea.

"I want to talk to you for a moment, honey. May I sit down and powder your feet while we talk?" She locked the door behind her.

"Mama . . . I can't even look at you. I have sinned so badly that I can't even look you in the eye," I cried.

"Bucky thinks he's in love, honey. He says you remind him of Frances Farmer, the old movie actress who had to have a frontal lobotomy. He told Daddy Snork and me that you were the woman for him." She pulled my feet out from under the bed sheets.

"Mama Snorkel?" I said as I lifted the pillow off my face. "Forgive me, but Bucky got laid—that's it. He's not in love. He just got a little unexpected pleasure during the wedding weekend. Don't hate me for deflowering your only son. I was very nice to him and I didn't throw up like I had expected." I pulled the baby-blue sheets up around my collarbone.

"I don't hate you, honey. I think it's lovely he was with you. I just wish you didn't have to be hung over to do it. He's a beautiful boy and things like that still mean something to him. He hasn't been with a lot of women. You have to remember that he just turned seventeen this past July." She brushed my toes with My Sin bath powder.

I was trying quietly to hide the bright orange Tang stain with the corner of the bedspread.

"Mama . . . I want you to know I would never hurt Bucky in any way. You have to know that . . . I think he's adorable."

"I don't want you to tell him you think he's adorable. I want you to let him know he's a man, a very special man," she said, patting my feet with her powdery hands.

"I will, I promise."

"Thank you, honey. It means a lot to me that he understands this whole thing from a woman's point and not from the boys in the repair shop. I know you'll say the right thing. And one last thing, Junie," she said as she covered my feet with the sheet. "I want you to stop drinking and get off the pills. They are making you a cloudy woman, honey. You are going to miss out on everything if you keep this up."

"Mama, I don't know if I can. I'm naturally a freaked-out person." There were tears in my eyes.

"I know you can't do it alone, honey. That's why I want the two of us to pray together and ask God for his divine intervention. I know if we ask him sincerely, he will give you the strength that you need."

Mama Snorkel and I held hands and prayed in silence. Her hands were soft and white with a firm, steady grip. I wished Sharon was with us to complete our prayer circle. Mama told me not to tell anyone I quit drinking and to keep it a secret between the two of us. She told me that over time people would figure it out for themselves. I never told anyone the date I quit the booze and pills—September 12, 1983. Mama Snorkel wrote it down on the cover page of the Bible she keeps by her bed. Every year she sends me an anniversary card.

When I came downstairs into the kitchen, Daddy Snorkel slapped Bucky on the back. "Here comes trouble, Bucky. You'd better run for the hills." He stuck his finger in my face. "Sharon ain't gonna like this one tiny bit, Junie-bird. She's gonna kick your ass when she gets back from her honeymoon." Bucky set a plate of scrambled eggs in front of me. "Now, Daddy, leave Junie alone. I promised her Sharon ain't gonna know nothin' about nothin'." The eggs were singed and dry, with too much salt. Cooked just the way I hated them. I swallowed them without chewing. "Here, Junie, eat this and I'll get you the Cream of Wheat when you're finished."

I left around dusk without saying good-bye to Daddy Snorkel. Mama stood in the white-pebble driveway and waved good-bye as she cradled her apricot-dipped toy poodle, Eclair, in her arms. As Bucky and I drove off in his brown, two-door Seville, I wondered if I was going to keep all of the promises I had made to her. When we got to the airport, we made out on the upper deck of the parking lot. I wasn't as shaky and hung over this time, and it felt so good to put my arms around his neck and kiss his soft, pink lips. It scared me to think about how much I was going to miss Bucky. He kept pulling me closer and closer into his chest. I wanted to collapse into him and lose myself more completely with each kiss. I was kissing him now. My panic and guilt had lifted and I was kissing him for the first time. He stopped being Sharon's baby brother. He started to put his hand up my blue knit skirt but I had to stop him. I was going to miss my plane. Bucky placed my hand on his chest for me to feel his heartbeat. He told me he was going to have to have a triple bypass if we didn't do it again—immediately. So Bucky got lucky a second time. He almost twisted my foot off when it got caught in the steering wheel. I boarded the plane with a red flush of whisker burn on my face. I wouldn't let him walk me to the boarding gate. We made out again by the rubber plants until airport security came by and told us to break it up.

I squeezed my eyes shut and kissed him on the forehead. I couldn't look at him when I waved good-bye.

During the flight I asked the flight attendant eight separate times for another bag of honey-roasted nuts. A little curly blonde-haired girl seated next to me asked me if I would give her a peanut. I told her no and went back to reading the emergency landing card. I thought the plane was going to crash from the thunderstorm we were flying through and I got a whopper of a panic attack. I reached for a tranquilizer and realized I had flushed them down the toilet back at the Snorkel ranch. I snapped off my safety belt, ran up through first class and locked myself in the bathroom.

I felt as if my heart was being ripped out of me, and I couldn't breathe. My head was spinning and I had to close my eyes to keep from passing out. I was dying inside. My throat was tight and dry. I couldn't swallow. I had just run away from the only person who would ever love me. I never told Bucky how much he meant to me. He never knew how deeply I needed him. It terrified me to realize how his simple kindness had touched me so deeply. I didn't know how I was going to get off the booze and the pills. Never in my life had I ever needed somebody to tell me that it was going to be all right. I sobbed into a couple of sheets of puckered white paper towels until the turbulence subsided. I rubbed my nose raw on the rough paper. My seat remained empty until the Fasten Seatbelt sign lit up. The captain announced that it was a rainy, sixty-eight degrees at the San Francisco International Airport. When I walked back to take my seat, the little curly-haired girl had fallen asleep using my jacket as a pillow. I snapped my seatbelt as tight as I could around my hips. My head throbbed from crying so hard. I couldn't breathe until I got back home to my apartment in Berkeley.

I graduated a semester early the same year I quit the

pills and booze. I gained fifteen pounds from eating Stouffer's frozen entrées. (Microwaves are very fattening.) Every day I was convinced that I would never make it to the following dawn. Most of the time I couldn't wait for my frozen dinner to take its final spin around the carousel. I would eat it with the edges bubbling hot and the center still frozen. The macaroni with Vermont cheddar cheese was my favorite. Shortly after graduation I moved to the Big Apple to become a writer—which is an enormously painful career when you have no safety nets. No pills or booze to soak up the flood of rejection and isolation. And so I made food my safety net. I became convinced that I was dying from a disease that doctors could not find. Loneliness is hard to diagnose.

It has been ten years since I've seen Bucky.

"Roland wants to know if you will come to a little mixer we're having Friday night at his place. He wants to set you up with one of his squash partners," Sharon said to me while going over the guest list with him on the phone.

"Squash? Who plays squash? I don't date guys who play *squash*."

"Oh, shush, and just go. Roland wants to know if you'll make some appetizers, something special," she said, getting back to her phone call.

"What's his name?"

"Paul Wollman, an investment counselor, forty-two, no kids, lives on the Upper East Side, wears only Eddie Bauer on the weekends, belongs to the Union Club, divorced for two years. . . ."

I gave an evil smile and probed the ultimate question: "Is he circumcised like Roland?"

"Forget it. You're not going."

"Good."

"Oh. . . . Roland says you have to go. Paul writes a lot of Op-Ed pieces for the *Times*."

"Then I'll hate him. Can't we do this another night?"

"No, I'm booked solid for the next two weeks," she whispered while covering the phone with her hand.

"Why can't we meet for drinks on Wednesday?"

"Roland and I are going to a NASCAR dinner with Bucky and his girlfriend. It has to be Friday night."

"Bucky's in town? What's Bucky doing in town?"

"I'll tell you later. Roland wants to know what you're going to bring to eat. He says nothing too fatty."

Nothing too fatty. . . . Give me a fucking break. Anybody who has the nerve to ask a guest to bring something and then tells her what to make deserves to have his eyes gouged out. I don't even know this guy and he's telling me what to do. I bet no one would ever talk to Martha Stewart that way. . . . Pisses me off. Now I have to figure out a way of getting the dirt on Bucky's whereabouts without making Sharon suspicious. What is Bucky doing with a girlfriend? He's supposed to be in love with me still. Remember me, the Frances Farmer of the cooking world? The Kim Novak of the Teflon set? (Bucky told me on the floor of the front seat that I also reminded him of Kim Novak in *Vertigo*. Bucky's sweet, but full of shit. He used to tell Sharon she looked like Victoria Principal whenever he wanted her to buy him beer.)

Now let me quickly say a few words on preparing seminomadic appetizers. It is best to make only appetizers that have a low casualty rate. Remember, it is better to forgo on originality than show up with something you have to ladle out of your purse because the Baggie burst. Two of my favorite appetizers to transport are walnut-Roquefort puffs and ricotta-artichoke pizzas made with pita bread. Both of these appetizers are unusual and are a breeze to transport. The walnut-Roquefort puffs are made simple by using Pepperidge Farms puff pastry. Just thaw the pastry and cut into bite-size pieces. Add a chunk of Roquefort cheese and top with a walnut half. Bake in a preheated 350-degree oven for 6 to 8 minutes and serve immediately. They are buttery and delicious and have a mellow, nutty tang to each bite. For the ricotta-artichoke pizzas, take a piece of pita bread, spread a layer of pesto sauce and then a thin layer of ricotta cheese. Add quartered artichoke hearts and sprinkle with pine nuts. Place pizza on a cookie sheet and heat in a preheated broiler for 3 to 5 minutes. Remove from broiler and cut pizzas into four large triangles. These little pizzas are easy, easy, easy and taste creamy and light with a hint of sweet basil. Other appetizers that travel well are Chinese marinated flank steak on skewers, bacon-wrapped chicken livers with sour green apple wedges, warmed new potatoes with sautéed onions in a curried mayonnaise and topped with black lumpfish caviar, and steamed asparagus tips with prosciutto wrapped in a herb cream cheese.

Most important, keep your assembly time to a minimum. It is also good to have a wide variety of appetizers to choose from. People will instantly realize what a clever cook you are. For Roland's little mixer, I think I will go with the ricotta-artichoke pizzas, the Chinese marinated flank steak on skewers, the warmed new potatoes with sautéed onions, curried mayonnaise and caviar, and the bacon-wrapped chicken livers with sour green apples. I usually make everything the night before and store it in airtight containers in the refrigerator. When I get to the party, I heat everything up and stagger the passing trays so people don't get hit with everything at once. I hate to bring anything to parties so I resent even having to talk about portable appetizers, but I do think they are an important art for a clever cook to master. People think that since cooking is my business, I must like to do it in my off hours. Now does anyone ask this of their gynecologist? They also like to pressure me into bringing complicated dishes from distant lands. Sorry, they've got the wrong girl for that. I like to bring food that is a little unusual yet not freakish and practical for me to transport. They don't hand out Academy Awards in my business, so I have no one to impress.

When Sharon got off the telephone with Roland, she insisted on seeing my menu of appetizers. If she thinks I'm bringing my own ice sculpture of a stuck pig, she is crazy. She sees entertaining like Jesus saw his Resurrection—it's a very big deal.

"Just tell me what you are going to make. Roland has a weak stomach," she said, unzipping her suitcase.

"Well then Roland can serve Rolaids at his little mixer. *So*, what is Bucky doing in town?"

"He and Daddy are sponsoring a stock car on the NASCAR circuit with some of Daddy's buddies. . . . Why don't you make cheese fondue?" she said, hanging her clothes in the hall closet.

"Fondue is out of style, Sharon. It's like the leisure suit of the food world. . . . So where is Bucky staying . . . ?" I asked, pretending to read the paper.

"He is staying at the Waldorf with his new girlfriend. Daddy decided to stay at home so he could bring her. . . . Why don't you make little Swedish meatballs in a brown gravy?" she said, pulling out her manicure kit.

"*No, Sharon.* . . . Swedish meatballs are the mood rings of the '90s. . . . So, what does Bucky's girlfriend do for a living?"

"She has a great little dress shop right outside of Dallas. . . . You'll meet her at Roland's mixer on Friday. They're going to stay the weekend. . . . What about serving oysters Rockefeller?" she said, sitting at the dining-room table and buffing her nails.

"*No, Sharon.* . . . I am not gonna wear some rubber apron so I can shuck oysters for Bucky's fucking party," I yelled, ready to strangle her.

"It's not Bucky's party. It's Roland who is giving the party. Roland. Remember him? The man I love and am trying to establish a new life with?" she snarled, jabbing the air with her emery board.

Busted. . . . I've been partially busted. I'm going to have to cool it with the questions. I've got four days to lose thirty pounds and get breast implants. Plus, let us not forget . . . make a hundred different varieties of hot appetizers. See, it's moments like these that I want to say: Don't ever get the reputation for being a good cook.

It is difficult to look good in your own home. Forget about looking good in someone else's when you have to bring appetizers. Now I can understand why wheels of Brie are so popular. You can just dump one on a plate with a couple of ferns and a box of stale Triscuits and forget about it. I'm going to take back everything I just said about what a breeze it is to transport appetizers. You can do it but you won't look good. Okay, I'm going to make the skewered flank steak, the ricotta-artichoke pizzas and the bacon-wrapped chicken livers with sour green apples and that is it. If Roland wants more appetizers he can ruin his own looks getting ready for his mixer. I have to look *fab-u-lous*. I am not going to be covered in chicken livers when I see Bucky.

I cannot tell you how many times I've brought fabulous food to parties and wound up trying to get Hawaiian Punch stains out of my cocktail dress while everyone else is strutting around looking like Zsa Zsa Gabor. Kim Novak would never allow herself to be shucking oysters in the bowels of the kitchen during a party. She'd be rubbing up against some international spy in a white tux. See, a clever cook must understand how and when to execute her craft in the kitchen. You can't be giving this stuff away for free. If anyone ever asks you to bring an appetizer or a dessert to one of the parties veto the

request with a big Nancy Reagan *no*. Just bring a jar
of macadamia nuts and wash your hands of the entire
mess. . . .

The night before the mixer I went down to Karen's
apartment to borrow one of her designer fat-girl dresses
that make you look thin. She and Steve had been fighting
ever since our dinner party and she hadn't gotten out of
her bathrobe in five days. She never went up to Woodstock. She never did the things on her list and she
canceled lunch with Evie. The only thing she had accom-
plished was reacquainting herself with her idol Natalie
Hunter of "All My Children." We ate Kentucky Fried
Chicken as I tried on her array of fat-girl-sucked-thin
cocktail dresses.

"This one makes my ass look too fat," I said, twirling
in front of the mirror.

"Yeah . . . it's not lookin' too good from the back.
Try the black one with the spaghetti straps. . . . So, are
you and Sharon getting along?" she asked, zipping up the
dress.

"This makes my boobs looks weird. . . . Yeah, I
never see her. She is always with Roland. She's helping
him redo his apartment. Where should I throw this?" I
said, nibbling the last bit of meat from a chicken wing.

"Just throw it on the floor of Steve's closet. . . . Yeah,
take that dress off. Try the black knit turtleneck with the
cutout shoulders. . . . Is Sharon screwing Roland yet?" she
said, helping me out of my dress.

"Nope, they come home from their little events and
sit on my couch like Dick Van Dyke and Debbie Reyn-
olds and he leaves by eleven thirty. . . . This dress isn't
too hideous . . . the lining is too tight around the hips
though."

"Here, we'll just rip the lining so it doesn't pull. . . .
Yeah, that will work just fine. . . . Just get a pair of black

Donna Karan control-top pantyhose and you'll look great. You want me to show you how to do your makeup?" she asked while she ripped the lining with her hands.

"Yeah . . . I can't breathe in this dress, but I can do that when I get home. . . . Who needs air? What are you doing this weekend?" I said, struggling the dress over my head.

"I don't know . . . Steve's gonna look for another place to live. I think I might just go to a bunch of movies by myself . . . I don't want to see anyone . . ."

"Why don't you have lunch with Evie and talk to her about things?"

"I can't do anything until I fix the kitchen in this apartment. I spoke to a realtor who told me I would lose a bundle if I sold it as is. . . . I've got to get someone in here to finish it. I don't know who would want to buy this place, it looks like a morgue," she said, sitting on the edge of her bed.

"Are you okay?"

"I'm just wakin' up to the reality of this situation, Junie . . . I'm just wakin' up."

When I got home from Karen's I put on a Frank Sinatra tape and went to work making the appetizers. From the looks of things Sharon and Roland had had a couple of glasses of red wine before they went to a dinner in honor of some judge. Sharon made cherry tomatoes stuffed with crab and bought some pâté with truffles. She's a very clever cook. To garnish the pâté plate she sliced oranges and draped fronds of fresh tarragon around the sides. Very chez nouvelle, Sharon! For the stuffed tomatoes she jeweled the plate with black and green olives. (She should have gotten pitted olives.) She even made her own croutons for the pâté. I was impressed. They were swaddled in a white linen napkin in their own little wicker basket. She even ironed the napkin—no flies on this girl. And she even had time to make my bed.

She and Roland got home around ten thirty. I had already changed into my lounging gear: black stretch pants with a man's wrinkled blue oxford shirt and sweat socks. I was up to my elbows in chicken livers and having a lovely time cooking.

"Junie? Junie, are you home? We've got a little surprise for you," she sang as she walked through the door.

"Yeah, I'm in the kitchen. What's my surprise? Did you guys bring me something to eat?" I yelled, pulling my hair out of my eyes.

"Well, I don't know . . . can you eat an entire hunk of gorgeous man in a navy blue suit?"

Oh shit, they brought that guy, Mr. Op-Ed man, back to my apartment for me to meet. See, it's times like these that I hate Sharon. She always gets me when I'm looking like death. If I ever brought a guy home when she wasn't in full drag, she'd cut my tongue out of my head.

"Are you dressed? Can we bring this fine specimen into the kitchen?"

"Sharon!" I buried myself in the refrigerator.

"Hi Junie. . . . How are you?"

"Bucky . . . Jesus . . . how are you? I didn't expect you—I would have brushed my hair." (Oh God, I want to die.)

"You look great, Junie, and you don't look hung over." He laughed as he leaned down to give me a hug.

"He said he just had to see you, honey, and I told him to just stop by right now. We all had drinks at the Oak Room." Sharon stuck her head in the kitchen. "Roland and I are going to let you two catch up . . . We'll be in the living room."

"What are you making?" He leaned against the wall.

"I'm making stuff for Roland's party tomorrow night.

I heard that you and your girlfriend were coming too. Why didn't you bring her by tonight?" I smiled, trying to take the edge out of my voice.

"Aw . . . I wanted to see you by myself first. She was real tired so she went back to the hotel with some friends."

"Oh . . . well . . . isn't that too bad."

It felt so awkward to see Bucky again. This wasn't how the story was supposed to go. You see, I was supposed to be at the party wearing Karen's tight black dress with these enormous breasts jutting out from right beneath my chin, standing in the center of a swarm of wild men. Then Bucky was supposed to enter—looking like he hadn't eaten since I got on the airplane. I'd wave to him across the party and he'd drop to his knees in a fit of tears and beg me to never leave him again. The girlfriend? Well, she would fall out of the cab on the way to the party and fall in love with the paramedic. (See, I'm not a bitch. I let her live.)

I don't know what to say about Bucky. He looked beautiful standing there in his blue suit and faded denim workshirt. I could see shades of Daddy Snorkel in him since he had shaved off his moustache. His face was more rugged and etched by the sun, but he still had his mama's soft pink mouth. He had gotten a lot taller and was much broader through the chest. Bucky still had that unassuming charm when he spoke. We stood in the kitchen and he helped me slip chunks of sour apple onto the toothpicks. He told me that Daddy had sold off a lot of the dealerships and they were spending most of their time going to stock car races. They traveled almost ten months out of the year throughout the South going from race to race. They were co-owners with a couple of other investors, but he and Daddy really ran the business side of the show.

"So are you having sex with all the pit bunnies?" I smiled and handed him some more toothpicks.

"No. I work really hard, Junie, I ain't got time for that. Besides they all want to have sex with the drivers."

"So tell me about your girlfriend."

"She's real nice. I haven't known her that long. Why are you so snoopy? . . . Gettin' jealous?" He stared right at me.

"I'm curious, Bucky. I just want to make sure you are happy."

"You don't care if I'm happy. You want to know if I'm getting laid."

"Well . . . I'm kind of perverted that way."

Everything was going great until Roland stuck his big boring beak into the kitchen and announced that he would drop Bucky back at the hotel. You want to know what Roland looks like? Go get any Harvard yearbook and open to the page with the class picture and close your eyes. Then take your finger and stick it anywhere on the page. There you go. That's Roland, totally non-descript. He could do a Revlon "Most Forgettable Man" commercial and it would be a total success—*because you'd forget him.* You want to know about his personality? Then take one slice of Wonder bread and soak it in a cup of low-fat milk for twenty minutes. There you go. You now have the psychological history of Roland's life.

Bucky turned to me as he was leaving and grabbed my arm. "I want to talk to you some more," he said. Sharon walked up to him and gave him a big hug. "Isn't he just the most gorgeous thing?" Roland and I both shook our heads in agreement.

After they left I sat on the floor in the living room and watched Sharon do her sit-ups in her Lanz flannel nightgown. I swear, I hadn't said more than three words to her since she arrived. She tucked her feet under the couch to anchor herself as she exercised.

"So . . . do you like Bucky's new girlfriend?" I asked nonchalantly.

"Oh please. He always likes the most screwed-up women. You know, Mama and I just shake our heads every time he brings another nut-job to the ranch. It's like he gets them off the locked ward from a state hospital."

"Oh Sharon, she can't be that bad."

"Trust me. He has a thing for run-over rabid blondes. . . . Don't you think Roland is really sexy?" she said, catching her breath.

"No. He's a twerp."

Run-over rabid blondes. . . . Sharon can be so goddamn vulgar. She really lacks a certain insight into people. The entire next day we argued about everything. She hated the dress Karen had lent me to wear. "It looks so obvious. This is a party for classy people, Junie. Can't you look classy just this once for me?" She hated the selection of appetizers I made. "Bacon? Didn't Roland tell you nothing fatty? And you have bacon wrapped around livers and apples? Can't you just do what he asked?"

To keep peace she decided to get ready over at Roland's apartment. When I arrived at the party she looked like she should be sitting on Santa's knee. Sharon wore a black velvet Empire-waist dress with a lacy princess yolk and patent leather flats with little black bows. She and Roland ran around the apartment putting coasters down on everything, including the toilet seat.

Paul Wollman, the Op-Ed man, arrived early to help me with the appetizers. He was another Harvard yearbook-type of guy only taller. He'd probably be pictured standing in the back row holding a billy club under his varsity jacket. I heated up the skewered marinated flank steaks as he recited his résumé. "Yes, I'm a Yalie . . . cum laude man." (What? Is he telling me he's into performing cunnilingus?) "I duck hunt and rock climb in my off hours. My function is to serve as a guardian to my clients' fortunes and protect the welfare and trust of their holdings . . . I'm a reader and I fancy myself as a gourmet man . . . Good palate . . . Good nose for wine and a good eye for women of breeding like yourself." (I think he's flirting with me. Probably thinks I'm into sodomy. I wonder what Sharon has told him?!) I said nothing to him for forty-five minutes as he watched me work my fingers to the bone. I just smiled and asked him to open the oven as I shoveled hot trays back and forth. He was kind enough to go to the bar and get me a diet 7-Up even though I had asked for a Coca-Cola with two limes. I spilled soy sauce all over Karen's dress and burned my hand on the side of the cookie sheet. I had pretty much rubbed all my makeup off my face while I was slaving under the hot, forbidding flames of Roland's broiler. As if I was cooking in the vats of hell itself as penance for my whoring ways. I ran my Donna Karan control-top pantyhose on the cabinet that contained the trash bags. "I'd lean down and get that for you myself but I've got a bad back—too much squash this week," he offered. (There is nothing worse than a yuppie scumbag.) So, as I earlier predicted, I looked terrible, but the appetizers were a huge success. I encouraged Paul to go out and greet the arriving guests with Roland and Sharon. Just as he was turning to leave he looked me dead in the eye and said, "I just want you to know that you are one of the most fascinating women I have ever met. I just love writers because they know so much about so many things." I had said two sentences to the guy: "Move, please" and "You are in my way."

What a fascinating woman I am.

Sharon pretended not to know me during the party so I started to introduce myself to Roland's guests as her best friend. She had made name tags for everyone. Roland's apartment was spacious with a large, uncomfortable burgundy leather couch in the center of the room. There was a maple coffee table, two green lamps, a painting of a horse and green plaid curtains. To spruce the place up Sharon persuaded Roland to buy a couple of tapestry pillows and a large tapestry rug and a maple dining room table. She had her work cut out for her. As it stood now, his apartment looked like a fraternity house yard sale. It was a good thing the room was crowded.

Bucky arrived late with his girlfriend, Angela. He had taken her to see the Broadway production of *Cats*. Angela was grossly overdressed but sweet in a paranoid sort of way. I liked her. I encouraged her not to eat anything if she felt as nauseous as she looked. She was worried that the waiter might have poisoned their food at dinner. Angela confided to me in the kitchen that she felt she was being followed by a guy in a turban driving a yellow taxi. I nodded sympathetically as she spoke. If I lived in Texas I knew we would be close friends. Bucky seemed a bit uncomfortable watching us from across the room. Once I started talking to her I found her to be very pretty. She reminded me of Linda Blair.

"What are you two talking about?" Bucky said as he grabbed my arm on my way to get another Coca-Cola.

"She's worried that she might have been poisoned at dinner. So I was helping her decide what the waiter might have poisoned her with." I smiled up at him.

"Oh yeah I know, she's been worried about that all night. She kept checking her pulse during the show. I told her we could go to an emergency room if she wanted to." He looked concerned.

"What's going on with Angela?" Sharon interrupted.

"I don't know. Why, is she sick?"

"Yes, I would say so. She's accusing Roland of having two-way mirrors in his bathroom. Will you go talk to her, Bucky?" Sharon demanded, storming off.

Bucky took off to find Angela and I returned to the kitchen to reheat another batch of appetizers for the crowd. Roland's guests were very complimentary about my wide selection of food on the trays. I was very happy to remain in the background working in the kitchen. This is one of the great things about being a clever cook: If you are shy or socially maladjusted you can meet very interesting people hiding out in the kitchen. Like bartenders and caterers are the most interesting people at parties. Another great place to meet interesting people is near the living room drapes. In fact, I met Karen behind the living room drapes at a birthday party. She used to not like to eat in front of people so she was snacking behind the drapes. People always make comments about what she eats—"You eat so much for a model" or "I thought models only ate carrot sticks." It used to make her self-conscious. I don't think she'd eat behind the drapes today.

Roland came into the kitchen to thank me for all of my help and to tell me that Paul would like to take me out for dinner next week. Paul told Roland that I needed to know more about him and figured a quiet dinner would be the best setting. I politely told Roland "no thank you" and went back to arranging my appetizers on the cookie sheet. It felt wonderful to be a powerful single woman again. It's great to get out and see how complicated people really are. I left the party quietly, slipping away unnoticed with my empty Tupperware under my arm. I was the happiest I have been in a long time. I can't really give a good reason other than I felt that I was just living my life.

When Sharon got back to my apartment she told me Angela would not be staying through the weekend. It seems she accused Bucky of hanging her mink coat on his side of the hotel closet. Angela felt there was a grand connection between the tainted dinner, the guy in the

turban following her in the taxi and the mink coat epi-
sode. She was convinced someone was trying to kidnap
her and Bucky was a part of the master coup d'Angela.
Bucky drove her to the airport early Saturday morning.
She gave him a long wet kiss by the flight deck and asked
him if he wouldn't mind being fingerprinted when he got
back to Dallas. Bucky continued to wave as the stewardess strapped her into the wheelchair and carted her onto
the plane. Angela was embittered about the fact that she
had failed to buy postcards of the skyline of Manhattan.
She never got to visit the Empire State Building for she
feared it was the national headquarters of her captors.
Life is rather stressful when you're a paranoid, flipped-
out, nut. What a pity.

Bucky and I are getting Polynesian food tonight at
7 p.m.

Life is weird.
    Time presses forward.
    Bucky is probably gonna get lucky. Again.
    —JUNIE

Walnut-Roquefort Puffs

MAKES 24 OR MORE PUFFS

8 ounces Roquefort
    cheese, crumbled
8 ounces goat cheese
¼ cup dry sherry
2 tablespoons chopped
    scallions

2 tablespoons chopped
    parsley
½ cup chopped walnuts
2 baguettes, sliced to ½-
    inch thickness

Preheat the broiler. Allow the cheeses to reach room temperature. Place them in a mixing bowl, add the sherry and blend, but do not smooth out the lumps. Add the scallions, parsley and walnuts and mix well.

Spread the cheese mixture generously on top of the baguette slices, set on an ungreased cookie sheet and broil until golden and bubbly, 2 to 3 minutes.

Ricotta–Artichoke Heart Pizza

SERVES 4 TO 5

½ cup pesto sauce
4 12-inch rounds of pita
    bread (do not split)
1 cup ricotta cheese
2 6-ounce jars marinated
    artichoke hearts

¼ cup pine nuts or
    walnuts
½ cup grated Parmesan
    cheese

Preheat the oven to 450 degrees. Spread a thin layer of pesto sauce onto each pita bread followed by a thin layer of ricotta cheese. Arrange the artichoke hearts and pine nuts or walnuts on each and sprinkle with a small handful of Parmesan cheese.

Place the pizzas on an ungreased cookie sheet and broil until golden brown, 4 to 5 minutes, or bake in the oven for 10 to 12 minutes. Remove from broiler or oven, place on a cutting board and cut each into four quarters. Serve warm.

Marinated Beef on Skewers

MAKES 8 6-INCH SKEWERS

¼ cup soy sauce
1 large garlic clove,
    minced
2 tablespoons sesame oil
2 tablespoons brown
    sugar

¾ pound sirloin tip steak,
    trimmed of fat and
    cut into 24 ½-inch
    pieces

Preheat the broiler. Combine all the ingredients, except the beef, in a mixing bowl. Add the beef and marinate for several hours or covered overnight in the refrigerator.

Thread beef onto skewers, with equal amounts of beef on each. Place them on an ungreased cookie sheet and broil 3 inches away from the flame for 5 to 8 minutes. Serve warm.

Bacon-Wrapped Chicken Livers with Sour Green Apples

½ cup soy sauce
¼ cup dry sherry
2 tablespoons honey or
    molasses
1 tablespoon orange juice
1 pound chicken livers,
    rinsed, trimmed and
    cut in half

½ pound bacon,
    uncooked
2 sour green apples, cut
    into ½-inch pieces

Preheat the broiler.

In a small mixing bowl, combine the soy sauce, sherry, honey and orange juice. Add the livers and marinate for several hours, or covered overnight in the refrigerator.

Cut the bacon slices in half and wrap around each piece of liver. Thread the livers onto skewers alternatingly with the apple wedges. (Each skewer can hold 3 wrapped livers and 3 apple wedges. If you don't have skewers, use wooden toothpicks with one liver and one piece of apple on each toothpick.)

Place the skewers on an ungreased cookie sheet and broil for 5 minutes on each side, about 3 inches from the flame, until bacon is golden and crispy. Serve warm.

Warmed New Potatoes and Sautéed Onions with Curried Mayonnaise and Caviar

SERVES 3 TO 4

10 to 12 small new pota-
toes, unpeeled and
halved
2 tablespoons butter
1 yellow onion, minced
½ cup mayonnaise
1 tablespoon curry
powder

2 tablespoons chopped
fresh parsley
Salt and pepper to taste
1 3-ounce jar lumpfish
caviar or the good
stuff

In a large pot bring 4 quarts salted water to a boil. Add the potatoes and boil until tender, about 12 minutes. Drain and allow to cool.

Melt the butter in a skillet on medium heat and sauté the onion until translucent. Add to the potatoes and toss.

In a small bowl blend the mayonnaise, curry powder and parsley. Add the mixture to the potatoes and toss, making sure that all the potatoes are evenly coated. Salt and pepper to taste and add the caviar. Skewer each potato with a wooden toothpick and arrange on a serving platter. Serve cold.

Note: This dish may be served as a cold salad for dinner or as an appetizer. It looks sort of weird but tastes great.

Steamed Asparagus
Wrapped in Prosciutto with
Herbed Cream Cheese

SERVES 8 TO 10

2 pounds medium aspar-
    agus spears (see
    Note)
¼ pound prosciutto,
    sliced paper thin

8 ounces of herbed cream
    cheese

Trim asparagus, reserving the tips only, 3 to 4 inches in length. Place it in one inch of boiling water in a skillet and boil for 3 to 5 minutes, or until tender crisp. Quickly remove from boiling water, rinse in cold water and dry with paper towels.

Cut each slice of prosciutto in half, lengthwise and set aside.

In a mixing bowl, stir herb cream cheese to soften, then gently spread a thin layer onto each prosciutto slice, making sure not to tear it. Wrap a prosciutto slice around each spear. Store in the refrigerator until ready to serve.

Note: Buy medium-size asparagus; thin spears are too flimsy for this recipe.

Dear Readers,

Junie asked me to give her something for the book that would give you hope and a desire to persevere. I pass along my favorite prayer, which I find possesses great wisdom.
May you know great happiness as a woman.

Carolyn Snorkel

ASKING PRAYER

I asked God for strength, that I might achieve. I was made weak, that I might learn humbly to obey.

I asked for health, that I might do greater things, but I was given infirmity, that I might do better things.

I asked for riches, that I might be happy. I was given poverty, that I might be wise.

I asked for power, that I might have the praise of men. I was given weakness, that I might feel the need of God.

I asked for all things, that I might enjoy life. I was given Life, that I might enjoy all things.

I got nothing that I asked for, but everything that I had hoped for.

Almost despite myself, my unspoken prayers were answered. I am among all men, most richly blessed.

Anonymous

Carnal Food

Well, we never made it out of his hotel room to get the Polynesian food.

Now, I realize if this were a Jackie Collins novel I'd be the head of my own movie studio by chapter 7. I would forfeit love for power and I would spawn with anyone who could access me to a higher plane of fame and social domain. Ego, Power, Power, Power, Ego. I would have sex with all the egos in Hollywood and not get seduced by my own yearning for a Nebraskan style of love. I would have left true love back with the Nautilus trainer, Brawny Dinkless, who broke my heart when he threw me over for the wife of a studio executive who had fat-injected breast implants larger than her fat-injected brain. I would discover them fornicating in the back of her two-seater gold Mercedes coupe parked on Rodeo

Drive while shopping for a dress to wear to a cocktail party given by the porn-star-turned-movie-producer Savage Dong. I would vow to the saleslady, Emelda, in Giorgio of Beverly Hills that I would seek my revenge by having sex only with my body and never again with my trusting heart. Sex would be my weapon against men. I would cut and slash my way to the top and wind up with an Academy Award for my movie about a beautiful, blonde, female police chief who pistol-whips Hispanic gang members into becoming vigilante farmers for the Brazilian rain forest. I would wear a brand-new Bob Mackie gown with each new phallus I conquered. My name would be something like Tiger Paw. I would apologize to no one for my power spawning or my calculated animal lust. Men would lick my heels as I stepped on their soulless faces. And the man who I really loved, the Nautilus trainer, Brawny Dinkless—the guy with the Michelangelo marbled ass—would be my pool cleaner, who I would force to scrub my tiles by using his tongue with a little Bon Ami cleanser. And the fat-injected wife of the studio exec, Tender Button, would be exposed on "Entertainment Tonight" for being a shallow, dopey slut with naturally dull hair. A plot revealed by the publicity department of my movie studio. I'd be a sadist with a heart of gold and earrings to match. Never would I, Tiger Paw, be seduced by love. Only power, baby . . . only power. . . .

So anyway, back to Bucky. . . .

When he phoned this morning he seemed anxious to get together. I was very suspicious. Why after all of this time did he want to see me so badly? . . . Possibly to bury his feelings for Angela?. . . . Possibly to get a free piece of ass on his way out of town?. . . . Possibly to cause problems between Sharon and me? . . . Possibly he had finally recognized his true feelings for me? . . . "No, Junie. It's none of those. I just want to see you because you are one of my favorite people. You are so funny," he explained, sighing into the phone. Hmm. . . . Why does he like me so much? Because I'm so crazy I make him feel so sane? Because I live in New York and therefore can never really get close to him? Because he can get a free piece of ass on his way out of town? (Funny how that keeps popping up?) Because I am a wonderful, loving woman who he feels accepts him for the emotionally limited but sweet man that he is? . . . "No, Junie. I just wanted to see you. Can't a guy just want to see you?"

What would Dr. Barbara De Angelis have to say about his answer?

"Why don't you go have dinner with him? Can't you just have dinner and leave it at that? Does every date have to be a great revelation to you? You guys don't even know each other, for Christ's sake," Evie said while sipping her cappuccino.

"I want to know what I'm getting into here and to protect myself from jumping into anything. Don't forget, I spent the last nine months in solitary confinement getting over someone." I hurled chunks of my bagel with cream cheese at the pigeons in Central Park.

"You want to protect yourself, Junie?"

"Yeah."

"Then don't have sex with him and wait and see what happens."

Evie and I had decided to meet in Central Park to go on an afternoon walk. Sol was getting on her nerves by acting like a Jewish mother hen. He wouldn't let her talk business on the telephone. He wouldn't let her do her Jane Fonda aerobics in front of the television. He wouldn't let her eat a bag of Fritos with her morning coffee while she read the *New York Times*. His mothering was also ruining their sex life. "He got all uptight last night when I wore the really sexy, lace red teddy to bed. Sol told me to put on my flannel nightgown. Then he told me we'd have to cancel the Playboy channel. He's worried that, God forbid, if we have a little steamy sex that something bad is going to happen to the baby. We've been married two weeks and he's driving me nuts. If I wanted to be treated like this I would have married his mother," Evie said as we paid the street vendor for the cappuccinos and bagels.

"Look, let's sit down on a bench. I can't eat and walk and talk at the same time," I said, juggling the coffee and bagel and my wallet.

The park was foggy and damp as we searched for a seat of our own. Every bench near the park's entrance was being used as a daybed for a homeless person. We didn't want to interrupt their solitude, so we sat near the children's playground. The dolphin-like shrill screams of the children playing on a jungle gym a few steps away made us both a little edgy. Motherhood and marriage were things Evie was going to have to come to grips with gradually. "If I could have planned this I would have given Sol and me more time together as a couple. This baby is rushing the whole process. I have got to sit down and talk to him about a couple of things. You know, Junie, it is crazy to fool yourself into thinking that it gets any easier once you are together with someone. It takes an enormous amount of compromise. When you are single, you can afford to be very selfish and self-righteous about things. Qualities that give you boundaries and independence as a single woman can ruin a marriage. For me to really make this relationship work I've had to erase a lot of boundaries in order to understand what Sol needs. And you know, I might be right about something but it doesn't mean shit in a relationship. There are no unbreakable truths in marriages, only opinions," she said, wrapping her fur-trimmed black leather coat around her.

You know, I hate going to the park. It's too noisy. I keep looking out of the corner of my eye for a pervert or a gang of thugs to bludgeon me to death. I'm so paranoid I can't even concentrate on what Evie is really saying to me. And worst of all, my toasted bagel is now cold and soggy and that fucking vendor put honey in my cappuccino—a waste of precious calories. Since I've been busy with Sharon, and Evie has been preoccupied with adjusting to all of the changes in her life, we haven't had a chance for a nice long talk. But I can tell by the expression on her face that she is going through a lot these days. As a committed woman, she has to learn how to stick around and choose her battles wisely. "Look, I can't yell at Sol when he tells me not to eat Fritos for breakfast now that I'm pregnant. It's his baby too. My body is not all my own anymore. I have to think of the two of them. I'm not used to thinking about other people. When I was single, I could blow off anyone who got up my ass. Sol tells me we've got to work together. I've never liked working with anybody on anything." She fell silent and watched a swarm of children playing in the sandbox.

It's confusing to think that all of the soul searching and inner strength that I have slowly, painfully been building throughout all my relationships are qualities that will need to be broken in order to let someone into my life. To make myself vulnerable again is to risk falling apart one more time. To go through the entire process again only to fail is a terrifying thought. The fear of losing myself again only makes it harder for me to make contact. My independence today only serves to separate me further from becoming a part of another person. There is a certain contentment in living alone as a single woman when you find your dignity. Feeding myself one hot meal a day and not dating anyone for a long time has allowed me to learn how to care for myself, no longer waiting for someone else to come along and give my life meaning and substance. I accept my aloneness as a way of life that isn't ruled from desperation and need. I am alone because I want to be a more courageous woman—not a sex object or a doormat, just a woman who respects herself, which is so difficult to do when you don't make a ton of money, or have multiple orgasms or a powerful social position. It is hard to make the world recognize the value of your aloneness. I have always just wanted to have some peace of mind when I walk down the street —alone. It may sound so simple but it is really quite difficult when everybody treats a single woman like her aloneness is a social disease. I always have people who want to set me up with someone, which is all well and fine, but the implication insults me. Why can't I just be single and not be made to feel like a marginal woman? Like I need a man or a child to give my life meaning? I don't know if I possess those qualities to become a partner with someone. I think my ability to live alone has become a real sense of my identity and I'm not so sure I want to give that up. "I don't think there is anyone around who is asking you to give anything up. He just wants to have dinner, honey," Evie interrupted. (Hey, I thought I was talking to myself for the past three paragraphs.) I know no one has asked me to give up my life, but up until now I never found my life as a single woman all that valuable. I was always waiting for someone to tell me I was worth something as a single woman. I guess more than anything that is what the past few months have been about. Slowly and carefully filling in those gaps in my psyche that told me I was nothing without a man in my life. When I started to feed myself. Just myself. The fever started to break. The panic of being alone has been quieted. . . . I am not waiting anymore. Now I worry about whether I *can* have a man in my life again. It all sounds terribly confusing listening to Evie speak about the man she loves. "Hey Junie, you're getting into one of your fatalistic fantasies again." (I wish Evie would quit butting into inner monologues.)

I saw Evie fight for her right to live alone as a single woman and have it feel like a contented place for her. And now she has to learn how to melt into someone and still continue to retain herself. To learn how to give self-lessly without collapsing into another faceless vacuum—to loose your identity as a woman in order to keep a man. I think this type of selfless giving is what trust is all about. To trust that kindness and caring are rewarded with equal treatment. A place where a woman's innate ability to nurture is recognized as a place of great strength and dignity. It takes enormous courage and trust to be a nurturing woman. A woman has to trust that her instincts will give her wisdom to know how to love someone and not wind up feeling drained and exploited by the whole experience.

Mama Snorkel would often talk about how Sharon fought to get a life after Sammy left her. Sharon tried a lot of careers and philosophies before she found her dignity. She is a very different woman today. I can tell by the way she treats herself. She wanted to find a man who wouldn't screw around on her. "Infidelity causes mental illness in a woman," she said to me this morning while brushing her teeth. "I'd rather be alone than put up with a man who can't keep his pants zipped up. I will never again tolerate a man who cannot respect the vows of his marriage. Life is too short."

I understand why Sharon doesn't jump in bed with Roland. (Even though the thought of Roland in bed with anyone makes me break out into one giant yawn.) I see how protective Sharon is about her singleness too. I doubt Sharon will ever overcome what Sammy did to her. Embarrassing her in public with other women, carrying on behind her back the way he did—it's as if he raped her soul when he did all that stuff to her. Her decision to have the abortion forced her to develop a new rela-tionship with God. One that taught her about forgiveness and compassion—which was what she needed in order to grow stronger as a person. You know, life either breaks you or makes you go deeper inside of yourself. In Sharon's case, it made her go deeper and emerge with qualities that I doubt she would have ever recognized. God is no longer some mystic forbidding figure to her. He revealed himself as a much more loving and enduring presence in her eyes. "Sammy was a blessing because he brought me closer to God. Tragedy deepened my under-standing of forgiveness. My abortion was a tragedy. I never thought I could go through with it, but I did and it changed me. It was the first decision I had ever made for myself, and I believe God gave me the courage to do it so I could get on with my life. . . . He gave me tre-mendous courage," she said last night before turning out the lights.

It began to rain lightly as Evie and I sat on the forest green park bench. Mothers quickly gathered up their chil-dren and packed up their toys and strollers. Evie pulled out her Versace tiger print umbrella with the gold-link tassel and snapped it open. "I hope all of those mothers run home, put their kids down for an afternoon nap, make themselves some tea and relax in a big cushy chair. See, I didn't used to hope for things like that until now. It must mean I am becoming a better person." She bal-anced the arm of the umbrella between us.

"Have you talked to Karen lately?" I asked, rolling a rubber ball back to a little boy in a red ski parka.

"I spoke to her this morning. Steve is going to be out of there before Christmas, she says."

"How do you think she's doing? I mean, do you think it's smart for her to move to Woodstock so quickly?" I asked, as the rain cleared the playground.

"Financially, she won't be able to do it until she fin-ishes the apartment and sells it. It's not a very practical apartment for its price. It's really meant for a single person who doesn't plan on having a family and that limits the type of buyer who will be able to afford it. She has got her work cut out for her. I also told her not to quit the modeling. Even though she doesn't work the way she used to, she still makes great money and it is going to be tough for her to find an income like that in another field. She's got to take her time and make some smart moves," she said, finishing the last bite of her raisin bagel with butter.

"I worry that she's gonna get stuck in a rut with Steve and the apartment and the whole modeling thing. You know, her work really makes her feel worthless because she competes with sixteen-year-olds. I mean who wants to stand next to skinny, young beautiful girls?" I said, shaking my head.

"Karen had enough brains and ambition to be a highly paid model for more than a decade and that's not just dumb luck, you know. She has many skills she can transfer into other things like beauty consulting or working for a fashion magazine or styling for photographers. She'll figure it out. I think she just needs people to listen to her right now," Evie replied.

"What about Steve?"

"Oh, fuck Steve, he's the least of her problems. She has known for a long time he is a pompous jerk. She's not trying to stop him. I think she would like him to leave sooner. It's his lingering presence that is driving her nuts. I mean they are just tearing each other apart this way."

"Yeah, I'll call her and see if she wants to come and stay with Sharon and me. All of us born-again virgins got to stick together," I laughed.

"Hey, if Sol keeps this no-sex stuff up any longer, I'll be moving in. I'm telling you, I am going home and telling him to get off my back and to treat me like a woman and not like a dumpy housewife. I'm not ready to be treated like his goddamn wife. You know, I feel swollen and puffy and my self-esteem isn't at an all-time high right now. I need to feel that he still wants me." She rubbed the drops of rain off her leopard print sunglasses.

"Yeah man, tell Sol to lighten up. . . . He should have been born a woman," I said, biting my thumbnail.

"I told him that the other day. I looked at him and said, 'You know, honey, if you keep this fussing and worrying up I am going to grow a dick so we can keep the yin-yang thing balanced between us.' "

In every direction the park was empty. The rain was falling harder, making the sand in the playground turn into a muddy shallow lake. Evie and I sat together staring out onto the lush, wet stillness. It's rare to hear such silence in New York City.

It was almost six o'clock by the time I got back to my apartment.

I showered and dressed quickly in order to meet Bucky at the Waldorf by seven o'clock. Luckily, Sharon was out with Roland—I didn't want her to see how nervous I was about having dinner with her baby brother. I told her this morning after he called that we were having a quick dinner before he left town. She gave me a quizzical look and said, "Is something going on here? He kept asking me at Roland's party if you were going out with Paul Wollman. I told him I thought you were too rowdy for a subdued man like Paul—he's quite the art collector. Paul told Roland he thought you were nice but a little autocratic. . . . You know, when I stop and think about it, you are just the type of girl Bucky falls for."

"You mean I'm a nut?" I said while slicing a sour green apple.

"Well, yeah. He likes birds with broken wings," she answered as she took a slice.

"We're just having dinner."

"Well, don't you even think about having sex with him. I'll know if you do."

"Sharon. . . . This is between Bucky and me now."

That last statement did not go over well. Sharon is still very protective of her little brother. Let's face it, we've been trying to ditch each other for years. The very idea of my becoming a family member makes her pantyhose shrivel up.

By the time I reached the hotel I was twenty minutes late. I rode the elevator up with two Japanese businessmen wearing matching black suits. They were very small and polite and bowed when I got off on the eleventh floor. I turned and bowed as I watched them disappear behind the closing metal doors. It was a very holy moment . . . I felt as if they were giving me a heavenly nod to go and fuck my brains out. And I returned the heavenly nod for them to do the same. Sort of a Hands Across the United Nations River of Lust. The passing of the international condoms zone. Very meaningful.

Bucky answered the door with a portable phone cradled by his ear. His white oxford shirt tails were clumsily tucked into his jeans. His belt was unbuckled and he has very tan feet with absolutely no mid-digital toe hair. I walked into the room and started to remove my dripping raincoat while he spoke with Daddy Snorkel. He walked up behind me and tugged the coat off my shoulders. "Sorry, I was trying to help you get this off," he whispered, while talking to his father. He was preoccupied with his conversation which calmed me down a bit. I caught a glimpse of myself in the mirror that hung over the maple writing desk. A bad hair night, no doubt about it. A frizzy, bad hair night. I walked into the bathroom while he continued his long-distance conversation. I toned down my frizzy mane by drying my hair with his travel dryer. I feel very guilty admitting this, but as I was combing out my split ends, I accidently peeked into his caramel brown leather shaving kit. The contents are as follows:

1 black-handled double-edged razor
1 travel-size can of Barbasol shaving cream
1 bottle of Neutraderm skin cream
1 bottle of Royal Lyme after-shave—with splash-on top
1 box of opened condoms, regular size—3 missing foil packets
1 box of unopened condoms, extra large (So which is he? Regular or extra large?)
1 tube of Colgate toothpaste
1 bottle of Mitchum deodorant—roll on (environmentally conscious)
1 black hair comb—purse size (with no white man's afro pick on the end)
1 bottle of Bayer aspirin
1 travel bottle of Flex shampoo
1 sterling silver toothbrush (a gift from a dopey slut, I'll bet you a hundred bucks)

Wait a minute—there is evidence loitering in the trash can. . . . Oh never mind. . . . It's a . . . (I'm bending over) a . . . an empty bottle of bubble bath, compliments of the Waldorf-Astoria. Hmmmmmmmmm. Who did he have a bubble bath with?????

"Are you drying off in there?" he said as he knocked on the bathroom door. I jumped when I heard his voice. I hadn't yet started retouching my makeup. I wasn't looking very good. In fact, I looked downright gruesome if you ask me, so I was trying to reconstruct an entirely new fashion look. Not an easy thing. "Oh hi. I was just . . . cleaning up a bit," I chirped as I opened the door. He looked so cute standing there leaning against the door jamb with his hand on his hip. He had this precious, dirty-minded-thirteen-year-old-boy of a smile on his face. So did I.

"So, you want to head out in this rain again? Or do you want to just order room service and watch a movie on TV? It's totally up to you, I am at your disposal the entire night," he said, leaning toward me, as he gave me a kiss on the cheek.

(Oh he has gotten to be such the Eric Estrada of manhood. What a fucking charmer. He's got that sweet, good ol' boy sex rap that makes you think he's not trying to do a thing but get you to feel nice and relaxed. . . . Like a slithering green garden snake with a banjo and a southern accent. He's flirting the way Glen Campbell probably would. Soooooooooo country-fried quaint about all this. I'm gonna make him beg for a while.)

"Yeah, we could just eat here if you want," I said, bobbing my head nervously. "We could do that." (Okay, I made him beg long enough.)

Bucky jumped up on the counter as I redid my makeup. His feet dangled in the air. "You don't need that. You look great with nothing on," he said as I lined my eyes with brown pencil. (Keep it up, Bucky, and you might see a breast before the shrimp cocktail.) He flipped open and shut the aspirin lid as I powdered my face. "You have a big, white, fluffy, fat kitty cat face—all soft and sweet." (*Did he say fat? Did he say I had an F.A.T. face????* I retract the breast; no breast action and not even a handshake after that slip.) I gave him the hairy eyeball on that last comment as I puckered my lips to gloss them with some Elizabeth Arden Brandy Frost. "I mean you have a pretty, full face like a kitty does, Junie. . . . I didn't say you were fat. You have those cat eyes and . . ." (Dig your hole deeper honey, go ahead, dig your hole a little deeper—no breasts or hand jobs. He blew it. Anytime a man slightly implies an issue with F.A.T. he can kiss his ass good-bye.) "Come on. I think you're the prettiest, smartest, funniest, brightest . . ." (Okay . . . maybe a half of a breast before dinner.)

Just a moment, please.

(Dear Mother and Dad:
I hope you are enjoying the book. Now would you please turn to the dessert section right this minute. The cooking tips are lousy in this chapter and so are the recipes. Just skip this entire section. Oh, and thanks for the check.

Love,
Junie)

Okay, let's continue. There's a sex scene coming. Let's just get my parents into the dessert section before I go full tilt. . . . If they read this part, they might ask for the check back. Oh, by the way, there is no dessert section, but it will keep them busy for a while.

Bucky followed me into the other room as I reached into the desk and got out the room service menu. "Order up a couple of bottles of champagne if you want, Junie." He is going in for the big kill tonight. He thinks I've forgotten about the F.A.T. remark, which shows you how little he knows about a modern woman. A modern woman will carry that word to her grave and his if she has to.

"Bucky, I don't drink anymore. Here, let's look at the menu."

Now men and women order food very differently. Men tend to order straight from the menu. No frills . . . maybe a subtle request for no butter or not too much salt, but a woman is a totally different specimen. Here, let me show you.

BUCKY'S DINNER

APPETIZER

Iced Jumbo Shrimp Cocktail
with traditional horseradish sauce $14.50
(I told you he'd get that)

MAIN COURSE

Charbroiled Black Angus Aged New York Sirloin Steak
Done: Rare to Medium-Rare $28.00
French Fried Potatoes
"no salt" $3.50
Creamed Spinach $4.75

DESSERT

Warm Pecan Pie with Vanilla Ice Cream
"No, I don't want coffee." $6.75

BEVERAGE

Amstel Light
Three bottles
Imported: $5.00 a beer

JUNIE'S DINNER

APPETIZER

Beef Consommé with fine herbs
"It better not have been made with any butter."
$5.25
Prosciutto de Parma and Melon
"Does that come with any rolls?"

"Yes, I want butter for my roll, but not in my soup."
$9.75
Mixed Green Salad, Vinaigrette
"No anchovies, but extra bleu cheese."
"Then, I want a side of crumbled bleu cheese."
$5.75

MAIN COURSE

Baked Potato
"Yes, I said I wanted both butter and sour cream."
"I can too have both."
$3.75
Creamed Spinach
"No, I don't want to share Mr. Snorkel's, I want my own."
"I will too eat it all."
"I'd like some Parmesan cheese sprinkled on top."
$5.75
Asparagus Polonaise
"I don't want it if it's made with butter."
"Oh, okay send it up."
"But bring me a side of sliced lemon."
"You will not need two carts. Just stack things."
$5.00

DESSERT

"Oh God, I can't eat dessert, I'm on a diet."
"What a crazy question."
"Wait a minute . . . send up a piece of cheesecake."
"No, I won't let you have a bite. Get your own slice."
New York Cheesecake
$6.75

BEVERAGE

Diet Coke
3 cans
$3.75 a can
"What do you mean you've never seen a girl
eat like this?"
"Well, then you've been dating transvestites."
"Yes, you have. . . . We do too eat. . . ."

Bucky stretched out on the cabbage-rose printed bedspread as he poked my ribs with his big toe. "So what do you want to do while we wait for dinner? Do you want to watch a movie? Hey, when did you quit drinking?" he quizzed while chewing the tip of a Papermate pen.

"Let's watch CNN. I'll sit in the chair. And I quit drinking over ten years ago."

"Why? Did you have a problem with it?"

"Well, I have a fundamental problem with life in general and I felt I needed to be as clear-eyed as possible to get through it," I said, smiling stoically.

"Was it hard for you? I mean, did you have a hard time not drinking?"

"Yes."

"Well, why don't you come here and tell me about it? You know you could have called me, Junie. Come here," he said, patting a place next to him on the bed.

I could hear Evie's voice screaming in my head, *"Get off that fucking bed this minute."* I crawled next to him and laid flat on my back. I said nothing. No man had ever asked me why I had quit drinking. I started to get tears in my eyes when I thought of all of the boyfriends that I had over the past decade who had never bothered to ask me what the problem was. Whenever I started to describe to them the relentless terror and madness that I woke up with every morning, I watched them slowly scoot their chair further away from me. Like my suffering was contagious. A lot of men like to hear condensed versions of personal tragedies. "Oh, wow, you must have been really screwed up." And the rest of the story was quickly suffocated by a queasy silence. Every time I felt that queasy silence I would say to myself, "Don't get into this, Junie, you're going to freak them out. Just keep it to yourself." I see that over the years of keeping it all inside, I have walled myself off from ever letting someone into my soul. I'd measure my words when I spoke so men would never see the cracks in my wall. It would be easy for me to blame this on uncaring men, but it wouldn't be an accurate statement. I stopped letting men know the shadows in my psyche when I started my romance with food. Food makes no judgment on failures in life. There has been something missing in my relationships for a long time. An intimacy is lacking. It has something to do with sex. Men don't have to work very hard to have sex with a woman anymore. They can have it without commitments or any feelings of obligation. I have underestimated how meaningful making love feels. I pretended I was a modern woman who could do it and walk away untouched by the whole experience. "Men don't like women who are downers. Be cheery and light. Ask them about sports." I don't know who said those words to me, but they have stuck in my craw from a tender age.

"You know, Bucky, some of us gals just ain't light-hearted, easygoing babes with firm butts. Some of us gals actually have a lot going on inside and it ain't all P.M.S.," I said staring up at the ceiling.

"I know that. Don't you think with growin' up with Mama and Sharon that I know women are . . . sensitive? You know, I can remember Mama when Daddy would be out with one of his girls, and Mama would just sort of

walk around the house with this frozen stare on her face."
He turned on his side to face me.

"And what do you think she was going through?"

"Well, I think she was going through a lot of things.
I think it embarrassed her because he was so public about
it for so long. I think it worried her that someone was
going to tell Sharon and me and I think it really hurt her,
as if she weren't a valuable person or someone you'd
want to be with," he said holding onto my arm.

"And what did it do to you?"

"Well, you know, I always tried to spend time with
her. She liked to talk while she worked around the house.
Daddy didn't spend much time at home. So I would talk
to her about stuff she liked to talk about."

"And what did it do to you?" I asked again, rubbing
his hand.

"I don't know, Junie. . . . I guess it made me hate
Daddy. I always felt like he never treated her very well.
Oh, I mean he gave her anything she wanted and never
yelled at her or hit her, but he just never seemed to want
to spend any time with her. You know Daddy can be a
real asshole. The only good thing that came from Mama's
cancer was that it got him to cool it with the chicks—I
think it really scared him that she might die first. You
might not think of it this way because she's so gentle, but
she is much stronger than he is."

"I know that, Bucky. Your mother is a very strong
woman. And so is Sharon."

"Yeah, well she's a lot different from when she was
growing up. I think Daddy spoiled her too much. He was
always really tough on me and he'd do anything for
Sharon. But Sharon's been through so much lately that
she's really had to grow up."

Room service interrupted our conversation. The bellhop wheeled in the cart piled with stacks of metal domed

plates. Bucky helped him set up the table near the corner of the room. I got up and looked out the window at the view of Park Avenue. The streets were black and slick, red brake lights glowed in the damp night. The window felt cold as I pressed my palm against the glass. "So are you ready to eat or do you want to wait for a while?" Bucky asked as he tipped the bellhop.

"Let's eat," I smiled.

I sat on the edge of the bed and gave Bucky the chair so he could have a good steady grip on his juicy Black Angus Steak. We had to put some of my side dishes on the floor to have enough room to eat. I traded him my asparagus polonaise for his creamed spinach. The creamed spinach felt silky and warm in my mouth. Bucky thought the asparagus was a bit overcooked. He ate a couple of spears and decided to move on to my baked potato. I squeezed a couple of slices of fresh lemon onto a succulent bite of steak and added a little black pepper before placing the forkful into his mouth. Steak tastes absolutely delicious when it has a juicy tang of lemon with some pepper. Bucky loved it and asked me to fix him another bite. "You are a great cook, Junie. This tastes fantastic. I'm always gonna eat it this way. What a genius you are," he said as he reached down and grabbed my ankle to remove my black suede loafer.

Bucky rubbed the arch of my foot as I fed him another bite of his lemon-peppered steak. He pulled my sock off and warmed my foot with his hands. I started to sigh as he picked up the baked potato with his hand and tore into it with his teeth. I drank my beef consommé by holding onto both handles. "See, you remind me of a kitty drinking milk from a saucer when you drink it that way," he said, winking at me.

Bucky scooted his chair over right next to me. He had sour cream running down his fingers and stuck them in my mouth to lick them clean. I bit down slightly on his index finger. "You can't have that. I need it to write my name with." Bucky leaned over and kissed my mouth. It was the lightest, feathery kiss I had ever felt—so tender. He moved slowly out of his chair and pressed me down onto the bed. I unbuttoned the top three buttons of his white oxford shirt. Bucky has a patch of hair on his chest in the shape of a tiny baseball diamond. His skin is very soft and tan. . . . I wonder. . . . "Bucky, do you go to a tanning salon?" I asked, interrupting our kiss. "No, Junie, I don't go to a tanning salon. Why don't we move up by the pillow so we can stretch out?" he said leaning up. I smiled at him as I pushed myself up near the pillow. Bucky always makes me smile. I flipped off my other shoe and put my foot down onto something cold and wet. "Ewwwww Gawd! I just stepped in something gooey, Bucky. I think I just mushed your pecan pie with vanilla ice cream. It's all over the bottom of my foot." I sat up. "Just take your sock off and get up here, right this minute," he ordered. I crawled on top of him and kissed the vein running down the side of his neck. My tongue tasted like scented lime oil. Bucky reached up the back of my black turtleneck sweater and tried to unhook my extra-padded push-up bra. "The hook's in the front, honey," I said, rubbing my nose against his. "God, it's easier to get into Fort Knox than to get into you, Junie. Why don't you take off your sweater and make it a little easier for me to touch you?" I sat up and removed my sweater, and Bucky unhooked the clasp with his fingertips. I reached down and unbuttoned the last four buttons of his shirt and helped him take it off. It felt so good to lie down on top of him with my skin touching his. He hugged me so tightly that my back cracked. "I just want to scoop you up and never let anything hurt you ever again, Junie. It breaks my heart when I see how badly somebody has hurt you," Bucky said as he rubbed my back. Tears slid down my cheeks onto his as he held me.

It was as if an unbearable sadness was being drained out of me. I had forgotten how wonderful it felt to be held by someone. Actually, I had not forgotten; it was having his arms around me that was the painful reminder of how easily it would be to slip and lose myself. To just fall into him and lose myself all over again. It is so painful for me to care for him and not feel like I am slipping back into that faceless void. I swing in such extremes. Either I'm surrounded by a thick, angry armor of fear or I'm suffocating in the arms of someone I deeply care for.

Even though I think I have a much better sense of myself, I am still terrified. It never gets easier, does it? I keep waiting for a time when there will be just peace of mind in my life. That's it. Just some peace of mind. I must go slowly . . . very slowly.

Bucky has this way of making me feel so safe and understood. We kissed for a very long time. If somebody were to ask me what I would like to do with the rest of my life, I would have to answer, "To kiss Bucky Langston Snorkel. I don't care if I never am a success in my career, I don't care about the rain forests, I don't care who is president, I don't care if I don't have slimmer thighs in thirty days—I just want to kiss Bucky, all day long. . . ." See, there I go slipping away.

At one point it started to get a bit steamy. My hand wound up on top of the silver buttons of his blue jeans. *"Don't you touch that!"* I heard Evie scream at the top of her lungs. It scared me so much that I jerked my head up. "What's wrong?" Bucky asked looking confused. "Bucky, I have to go home now. I can't stay any longer. I don't want to get anything started that is going to make me miss you any more than I do right now. I haven't been with anyone in a long time and I can't jump back in like this. I can't do it anymore. I just can't," I said rolling off of him.

(Hey, don't get mad at me 'cause I had to cut the

juicy sex scene. Let me tell you, it was fabulous. Absolutely fabulous. I wish you could have been there. I wish every woman could have a guy who kissed her the way Bucky kisses. It beats the hell out of cheesecake. I would have gladly gone on for another hundred pages of just raw carnality. Or is it carnalingus? You want to blame someone? Then blame Evie, she's the one who blew this chapter.)

Bucky seemed very hurt and confused by my decision to not spend the night with him. "I don't understand why you always run away whenever there is a moment for us to be together. It drives me nuts, Junie," he said pulling on his shirt.

"Because, Bucky, I can't be with you and walk away. I can't, I am not built that way."

Bucky sat down on the bed next to me. "So, what do you want from me?"

"I don't know, Bucky, I don't know what I want. I guess I just want a chance to know you. To see if I could know you. We don't even know each other," I said, leaning my head on his shoulder.

"Well, are you saying you want to see me after tonight?"

"Ummmmm. . . ." (I feel sick to my stomach and I'm getting a headache.) "Yeah, but it's not gonna work. Sharon will have a cow. You live in Texas and by the way—what about Angela? What are your feelings for her?"

Bucky got up from the bed and walked over to the chair and sat down. He seemed to resent my grilling questions. "Angela and I are not going to be seeing much of each other anymore. We didn't get along very well. I don't think she trusts me very much."

"And why was that? Did you try to have sex with her sister or something?" (I shouldn't have said that. He just glared at me.)

"Junie, you can be so sick at times. She'd had some bad relationships with men and was very pushy about wanting me to get very involved with her before I was ready. I didn't want to be pushed into a relationship with her. She was very jealous and I couldn't take the constant accusations. I just wanted to go out with her—not have her baby for Christ's sake."

"Don't you miss her? I mean, isn't it hard for you to be with another woman so quickly? Don't you need some time to sort out your feelings?"

"I sorted out my feelings today on the way back from the airport. And I came to the conclusion that we are best off not involved with each other . . . it was never easy with her."

"So let me get this straight. You need one day to get over someone you made love with three times in four days?" (Oops, definitely shouldn't have said that. He's staring at me trying to figure out how I know they had sex three times since they've been here.) "I mean, I'm assuming you had sex three times in four days. A random number. . . ."

"I'm not talking to you about Angela. I'm over her."

"Well, excuse me, Bucky, but I'm not over Angela and I need you to talk to me about her," I said, sticking my finger in the cheesecake and licking it clean.

"Junie, do you want to be with me? Is that what this is all about? I don't understand why you are asking all of these questions unless you are trying to figure out if you want to be with me or not."

"Yes. There I've said it. Yes, I would like to be with you. *But*, and there is a *big but* to this, I need time, patience and enormous understanding and you have to talk to me. You can't just ignore me—you have to talk to me."

"I'll always talk to you, Junie," he said, looking exhausted.

Okay, so to make a short story long I spent the night

with him under the condition that we did not have sex. Well, nothing below the waist, and I felt I was being very, very generous in my negotiations. Bucky shook his head and rolled his eyes a lot and kept on saying, "I'll respect you in the morning. I respected you the morning after we did it at Sharon's wedding, didn't I?" Hey, wait a minute—Bucky told me that we didn't do it the night of Sharon's wedding. I was always under the impression that we didn't do it until the next day. "Nope, we did it in the laundry room behind the margarita machine. I knew it would freak you out so I decided to wait and tell you when you weren't so guilt-ridden." So the big moment when Bucky lost his virginity I guess I witnessed in body but not in spirit, so to speak. "What was it like? Was it the single greatest experience of your entire life?" I asked.

"It was quick, babe—very, very quick."

Bucky handed me an old T-shirt and a pair of sweatpants. "Here Junie, get comfortable. This is really stupid, but if it will make you feel better then we won't do it." I went into the bathroom and ran the water in the tub. I squeezed the entire bottle of Flex shampoo into the water and hit the whirlpool button on the side of the wall. I was stressed out and needed to gather my thoughts, which I do best in the bathtub. The whirlpool made the shampoo explode into a volcano of bubbles. Bubbles cascaded down the sides of the tub, over the faucet and into the soap dish. I took off my black knit pants, my extra-padded push-up bra, my black lace underwear. I looked at myself standing naked in the mirror. My ass is dropping—crashing to the floor is more like it. My breasts look terrific in the push-up bra . . . I'm never taking it off. If someone ever dared to rob me I'd tell them, "Take everything but the bra. Here's my dad's Visa card. I promise not to call him for a couple of days. Just leave the bra—I'll die without it." I'm a wreck. He is definitely not seeing me without a lot of blue gauze and candles. *No overhead lights.*

I dropped into the tub and watched the swirling water cup me in hundreds of tiny bubbles. They were flowing onto the white tile floor. It felt so good to soak in the boiling hot water. I put a wet white washcloth over my eyes. Hang on a minute . . . Bucky's knocking on the door. I have to strategically place my bubbles so my breasts look enormous . . . lots of cleavage. . . .

"Oh God, Junie, what have you done? You've got bubbles everywhere," he said, looking down at me.

"So can't a girl take a bath? You got a problem, Bucky?" I pulled the washcloth off my eyes.

"No, I don't have a problem. But can't a guy take a bath with a girl? It's lonely out there. Why don't you just let me crawl in and I'll wash your hair," he said with his big moon-doggie eyeballs.

"Oh bullshit, you will not. You'll crawl in here and want a hand job or something—I know you dirty dogs. Are you wearing boxers?" I quizzed.

"Yeah. You want me to wear my boxers, Junie? You want me to look like an idiot?"

"There will be no displays of genitalia the entire night—that's the deal. And besides, you are only going to look like an idiot in front of me," I smiled.

Bucky took the no Frills 'n' Thrills offer and crawled into my cloud of bubbles. We kissed and kissed. He told me stories about the first time he felt a girl's breasts. "They were the softest most beautiful things I had ever felt in my entire life. Just like yours." (This boy learned how to cover his ass by including my breasts. Savvy, Bucky my boy, very savvy.) Then he went on to tell me how girls always wanted him to talk more about his feelings. "I don't know, when I like a girl, I just like her. I don't really think a lot about it. I just like her, ya know?" (Okay, so Henry Miller he is not.) Then we kissed some more and some more. He got some breast action . . . or I got some breast action. He washed my feet. I scrubbed his back. He washed my hair. I massaged his feet with hair conditioner. He told me when he was on a Boy Scout camp-out when he was thirteen, he confessed at the camp fire that he was in love with his pet cow, Rosie, and no one would share a tent with him the rest of the trip. (Okay, so he's an animal lover. So was Marlin Perkins. But, isn't thirteen a little old to be in love with a cow?) Oh well . . . we kissed some more . . . we kissed until our fingers looked like blueberries.

By the time we shut off the lights it was two in the morning. We lay side by side and listened to the couple in the room behind the bed screwing their brains out. "God, is she having a great time or what? I've never heard a girl moan like that," he said, holding my breast in the dark.

"She's faking it," I answered, rubbing cream on my face.

"No she ain't. She's screaming like she's never had it so good. God, no one's ever screamed like that with me." He sounded so disappointed.

"That's because no one has faked it with you. Nobody makes that much noise unless they are faking it. She's faking it. Wait . . . now you can hear him . . . he's moaning. God, he's really moaning. He's faking it—that's a fake moan." I wrapped my arm around his waist.

"Junie, he ain't faking it—that's the real thing. He's pitching his tent as we speak. He definitely ain't faking it," he announced while tangling his feet in mine.

"Well, she is," I said as I kissed him good night.

There was one couple staying at the Waldorf-Astoria who had great sex that night and there was another couple who got a great night's sleep. Anyone like to take a guess on which one we were?????

I was delightfully awakened by Bucky kissing the back of my neck. I could feel his whiskers rubbing against me. It felt great. I pretended to be asleep as he rubbed my back. I woke up smiling. It felt so great to be curled up with him in crispy white cotton sheets.

"God, Junie, I'd give anything . . . just to. . . . Come on, Junie, just a little," he begged in my ear.

"There will be no display of genitalia in this bed, Bucky. You will have to take matters into your own hands," I said in my Evie voice.

He rolled over and rubbed his eyes, "Goddamn it. I'm gonna go shave. You are such a drag, Junie—you can be such a drag when you want to be."

After he showered and shaved he was in a little better mood—not a lot better, but at least he smiled at me when he packed up his suitcase. He even let me order breakfast. "You have to eat everything you order this time, Junie. Last night was a bust."

What a nag.

BUCKY'S BREAKFAST

Two Eggs Any Style
"Scrambled"
$7.50
Whole Wheat Toast
"Yeah, butter's fine"
$3.75
Fresh Orange Juice
$4.50

JUNIE'S BREAKFAST

French Toast
"No butter, but extra syrup and powdered sugar."
$10.75

Apple Juice
"Are you sure you don't have any grape juice?"
$4.50
Large Pot of Coffee
serves: 6
"I will not have a panic attack."
"I'll need half 'n' half."
"If you send milk, I'll send you back downstairs."
"Yes, that is a threat."
$7.00

I started to cry as I showered and got dressed. I looked like I had been slapped and buried and then dug back up. I didn't want to say good-bye to Bucky. This is what I had been dreading the entire night . . . I hate to say good-bye. Bucky was running around so he could catch his two o'clock flight back to Texas. "Don't cry, will you just not cry. . . . Oh God, Junie . . . please don't cry," he said as he ran to let the bellhop in with our breakfast.

"I can't help it," I sobbed. "I'll see you again when you are in the hospital having a colostomy and I won't have any of my own teeth. Wait—I'm older than you—you'll come to visit me when I'm having my colostomy and you'll have no hair."

"Stop this right now. You're coming to the stock car races in Atlanta in two weeks. I'm gonna send you a ticket. Now eat your breakfast. Don't drink too much coffee and get all flipped out, okay Junie? Not this morning."

"Sharon's gonna kick my ass when I get home and you're going back to Angela 'cause she'll have sex with you," I wailed into my french toast.

"Don't start with this. Angela is done. I told you that last night. I'm gonna call Sharon tonight when she's at your place. I'll handle her. Just don't start any fights with her before I do. Now Junie, just eat your breakfast."

"You're going to ignore me at the stock car races—I just know it," I said, stuffing the whole slice of french toast into my mouth.

"If you start this shit, I will. And another thing. . . . You better bring some birth control because you are going to be putting out all weekend long," he said, shoving his eggs into his mouth while he finished packing.

"I might not be ready."

"You have two weeks to get ready. Now stop being so bossy, Junie. There are two of us here and I'm gonna be ready to have sex. So just get used to it."

"Don't push me around. I have my own identity. You can't push me around, honey. I think you have an inner hostility toward women, Bucky. You might want to look at that," I sniveled.

"Junie, I've got an inner hostility toward you, not women. You are trying to wreck this with all this weepy bullshit. Call one of your girlfriends when you get home. I've got to catch this flight. I'm not gonna analyze this with you. Just call a friend and tell them how much I hate women and when I call you tonight you can tell me what they say."

We went downstairs together. I watched him as he checked out at the front desk. I am sick to my stomach. This is never gonna work. I'm not ready to have a relationship. I'm too screwed up to be in a relationship. I'm doomed. Bucky walked up to me and stuffed both of his hands into the pockets of my raincoat and gave me a passionate kiss in front of all of these Japanese tourists. "I'll call you tonight before I go to bed," he said as he kissed my forehead.

"No you won't, you'll forget about me as soon as you see a stewardess in a tight skirt," I said with tears in my eyes.

"Junie, I'm gonna miss my plane. I will call you tonight. Look in your pocket after I leave. Junie, don't cry.

Don't let the last look I have at you be of you with tears in your eyes. Now don't," he said, hugging me.

I waved good-bye as he jumped into a cab. I walked home in the rain and cried the entire way. This will never work. . . . It's doomed like every other relationship. I'm going to get squished like a bug on a windshield. He's a lying sack of shit . . . I'm yesterday's news . . . He's probably having sex with the cab driver right now . . . I hate his guts . . . He's a snake'n dog just like his Daddy. Oh wait a minute, he told me to check my pockets.

Dear Junie,

I don't know why, because you drive me crazy, but I have always loved you.

Now stop crying,
— Bucky

Isn't he the most wonderful man to walk the face of this earth?

Author's note: I was planning on writing about the wonders of shellfish in this chapter, but frankly my dear friends, I've got bigger fish to fry—a Bucky fish. Just heat up a box of Mrs. Paul's fishsticks and forget I ever mentioned it.

Isn't he just the most beautiful man????

Uh — hi:

I'm Becky Snorkel and Junie wants me to put something in her book about being a clever cook. I have no idea what she is talking about.

I don't understand all this stuff about food and emotions and feelings... I think she should just keep her big mouth shut and have sex with me.

Somebody tell her to lighten up.

Ten hints for Junie and her clever cooks:

1. Stop snooping through my shaving kit.

2. Don't interrogate me about my past relationships.

3. Have sex with me whenever I give the signal.

4. Don't wear sweats to bed. Wear something with garter belts.

5. Think about, but don't dissect, my every word.

6. Don't ask me to read John Bradshaw or that Ironlew guy.

7. Don't be so bossy. Let me finish my own sentences.

8. Stop whinning and cut out the crying every time I get ready to leave.

9. If you are having one of your mood swings, call a girlfriend.

10. Have sex with me without asking me to commit my left testicle.

PS Junie: memorize this list before you get on the phone for Atlanta. You were starting to get on my nerves after the bubble bath.

—Bucky.

Lettuce Forgive and Forget

*T*hank God . . . I can greet another day. . . . King Tut
has spoken.

Bucky faxed me his clever cook's hints after our
phone conversation. The warm romantic glow of our
night together had worn off by late Sunday night when
he called. "Hi. Put Sharon on the phone so I can talk to
her. I hope you two haven't made this into a big deal,
Junie. . . . Junie? Have you made this into another melo-
drama? Don't answer that question, just put her on the
telephone."

Sharon snatched the phone right out of my hands.
She practically strangled the air out of my lungs when
she yanked the cord from around my neck. "Oh shit,
Sharon, why don't you go listen to one of your Anthony
Robbins tapes and anchor down your personality," I

snapped as I rubbed my throat. Sharon turned around and hissed right back at me, "Why don't you go listen to one of my Anthony Robbins tapes and quit screwing my baby brother, you two-faced slut."

Can you believe that stupid bitch had the nerve to call me a two-faced slut! She is so fucking vulgar. I mean, really.

Those were the first words she spoke to me the entire day. Sharon was an industrial-strength, mega-ton, full-throttle, one thousand-pound cow all day long. She gave me the silent treatment, slammed a lot of doors and muttered things under her breath, like, "Lying, conniving bitch . . . can't keep her paws off of him . . . rubs it in my face . . . Roland's probably next." Really nice remarks from a childhood friend, huh? (And I'm downplaying her reaction in case there are young children reading this book.) I left the room so she and Bucky could speak more openly about deep and sensitive *me*. But I listened from the keyhole in case Sharon has the nerve to air any of my dirty laundry. (If she dares to tell Bucky that I had sex with my statistics professor so I could graduate from Berkeley, I am going to tell Roland that Sharon let a guy named Spooky from Spokane, Washington, take naked pictures of her during her Cleopatra years. The reason we called him Spooky was because once, after they had done it, he sobbed into her black pharaoh-style hairdo and confessed that she reminded him of a gal named Doris, his mother's standard poodle, whom he loved, but pretended to hate in order not to make his mother jealous. Spooky, right? Really, really Spooky.)

Sharon threw open the door and shoved the phone in my face when she had finished her conversation with Bucky. "Here—I wash my hands of this entire mess. Congratulations. He's head over heels and wants to make a go of this nightmare. I'm going to stay with Roland. This is more than I can handle," she thundered, throwing my raincoat over her flannel pajamas.

A pack of vicious lies. Lies that I will not even deign to substantiate with a moment of self-reflection. I did not chew him up and spit him out. And the bit about my father bailing me out . . . well, okay, that's kind of true but she had no right to blow my artistic cover. Hey, I already told you about the statistics professor, so get that look off your face. I never claimed to be a Rhodes scholar. (I'm a little worried someone from N.O.W. might ask for my membership card back. They don't endorse things like screwing your way to the top when you are a woman, but I didn't get to the top. He only gave me a B–.) It was really stupid and I felt like a real whore for doing it with him, but he was a real whore for giving me the B– since all things considered, I deserved an A.

The tougher and more aggressive I am on the out-side, the more desperate and needy I am on the inside. My desperation made me think I was tough enough to have sex with a man for a lousy grade. I lied to myself when I fooled myself into thinking that I could do some-thing like that to get ahead in life. Karma has a way of handling bad judgment though. It is situations like the one with the professor that separated me from my in-stincts in the first place. Anytime I have used sex for any-thing but love there are unintended consequences that left me feeling somewhat separated and fraudulent in-side. It goes against the very nature of who I am. The first time around the bend with Bucky I used him to soak up my loneliness and desperation. Just like a drink or a pill or a large, drippy spoonful of Cherry Garcia ice cream. I used him to find that piece of me I buried a long time ago. Sex, food, men—it can all become so distorted so easily. A front of toughness can really damage people you never intended to hurt, which makes me feel ashamed of myself. To use my sex for personal gain, or

MS. SHARON SNORKEL LOVIT

Dear Sweet Lovely Readers:

I am sure you are wondering why I am so upset that Bucky and Junie are together. Well, let me tell you a few things about Junie that I am sure that she has failed to mention. Namely, her track record with men reads like the Sunday obituaries. She thinks I don't know that she goosed Bucky at my wedding. Do you know how many people saw them in the laundry room behind the margarita machine? The laundry room was to the right of the dance floor . . . Everyone saw every birthmark, tattoo, ingrown hair, you name it. Junie blew him off the minute she got back to Berkeley so she could get back to screwing her statistics professor. Poor Bucky was devastated when she laid him and left. He moped around the ranch thinking that he had done something wrong. **HE WAS SEVENTEEN YEARS OLD FOR CHRIST'S SAKE.** *He left messages on her machine and she never returned his calls. She chewed him up and spit him out. And she will do it again.*

Oh, and this business about her being such a tortured writer? Well, if it wasn't for her father, Mueller C. Lake, bailing her sorry ass out of financial ruin every six months, our dear Junie would be writing her cooking columns from Leavenworth federal prison right now. So her suffering has been in a pretty cushy setting. Mueller Lake was just so grateful when she quit boozing and making such a public ass of herself that every time she threatens to hit the bottle again, he pulls out the checkbook. Mueller pays her off to preserve the family name. So don't think Junie's some wandering waif in the streets of New York. She's got a profitable racket going here.

If she breaks Bucky's heart one more time, I'll kill her.

> *Call me and I'll fill you in on the rest.*
> *All Hugs & Kisses*

> *Sharon Snorkel Lovit*
> *Don't forget to call me if you come to Dallas!*

for trying to fill in those gaps in my psyche, left me feeling like a fake. Since I had no personal relationship with my professor, I channeled my feelings of guilt into my relationship with food. Which served to only separate me further from any real human exchange. As for the early days with Bucky . . . a casualty of a woman at war with herself.

I've been born into a world that strips a woman of her instinct to nurture, which leaves me combing the universe for a place for my soul to nest. I have given so much power to men by fooling myself into thinking that it is more important to nurture them over myself. I know now that my power is born within my ability to take care of myself. The power of my own self-respect makes me value my life as a single woman. When I nurture myself I am free to nurture the world around me. No longer do I have to live through food to make me feel safe and protected. That is why Bucky isn't afraid of a powerful woman. Mama Snorkel showed him the power of her ability to nurture by using her God-given femininity and he felt secured and loved. (Okay, so his dad fucked him up a bit with his relentless philandering, but Bucky isn't afraid of a woman's ability to nurture.) If you were to meet him in person, you'd see what I mean. When I put my arms around him, he responds with such gentleness. He can cook for a woman and not feel emasculated. He can let a woman feed him and find it sensual and engaging. He can allow a woman to be a woman and not feel as if he is being swallowed whole. My feeble attempts to nurture him do not make him feel suffocated, which is what I think men felt from me because I was unable to care for myself. My need for some morsel of love was too overwhelming. It left me starving to death inside.

The other way I used to cope was to remain cold and aloof, insuring that men never witnessed my vulnerability. Which starved my relationships to death emotionally, while I stuffed myself with food to try to penetrate that chronic isolation I always felt with men. I appeared so tough and self-sufficient, yet was so fragile and empty in many ways. I would have sex with men, but would make sure they never knew me, starving myself from any real sensuality. Or starving men from knowing my vulnerability and stuffing myself with food as a way to not feel so terrified and alone.

I did Bucky a favor when I released him back into his adolescence to gather his manly ways in the world. I vaguely remember a few phone messages from Bucky, but for me to speak to him back then with all my sores open and weeping would have crushed the armor around my heart. When I got back on the phone with him I recognized what it is I love about him—his sense of the present. He is very present and consistent in his feelings for me. Bucky doesn't cut himself off from his feelings. He has always let me know that he cares for me. Bucky doesn't become distant and aloof after he has been intimate with me in order to remain in control. He remains constant. "Junie, just leave Sharon alone so she can get used to this. I'm going to send you some plane tickets for the race in Atlanta. I won't be able to meet you at the airport so take a cab to the Lemon Tree Motor Lodge. . . . I'll send you the address. Now I send you a big kiss good night and I'll call you in a few days—and *don't start any trouble.*"

"Hey Bucky—you want to have phone sex?" I whispered seductively.

"No, Junie, I'm afraid you'll have a mood swing and leave me in a backhanded clutch at the finish line. You always do that to me. . . . That's gotta stop, babe," he sighed.

Well, so much for that idea.

I immediately called Mama Snorkel after I hung up with Bucky. During the day when Sharon was cowing around my apartment acting out her own Greek tragedy, I overheard her telling Mama that I had spent the night with Bucky. Unfortunately for me, Daddy Snorkel answered the phone. "I told Sharon to get a gun and shoot ya dead in some dark alley," he cackled.

"Gee, Daddy Snork, how kind of you."

"Ah, since the day I laid eyes on you I could tell you were a bad seed. I'm with Sharon on this. And let me warn you, young lady, you scramble Bucky's brains around like you did the last time and I'll come up there and shoot ya myself. Now here's Mama."

As always, Mama Snorkel was wonderful about this sticky situation. When she got on the telephone she listened to me bitch and moan for twenty minutes straight without saying a word. "Honey, I think you are missing the point. Sharon is extremely hurt that you have not been more supportive of her relationship with Roland. She says you are very rude to him and never ask her anything about the two of them. She says you've gotten to be very selfish. Is that true, Junie? Have you gotten to be a selfish person?"

"You know, Mama, I love Sharon. It's just that we're such different women. Sharon is just so . . . so . . . cautious and controlling all the time. I don't know how to be her friend anymore."

"Honey, she is just trying not to repeat the same mistakes. You should remind her of how strong and loving she has become. She needs to be reminded of all that she has given to herself over the past few years. And you are just the person she would believe if you said it to her. I want you to be more thoughtful of Sharon and all that she has been through. And I told her to do the same with you, Junie. She is just as scared about getting close to a man as you are. You both could really use each other's friendship right now."

"You're right. I've been terrible to Sharon. I'm gonna think about what you said."

"Junie, I want you to work on having some faith in yourself. I want you to be more considerate about what other people are going through. You're scared. Sharon is scared. And Bucky is scared. He doesn't know how to make you trust him and it scares him that you are going to hurt him again. You don't have to fight so hard anymore. You don't have to protect yourself so much, angel."

"I am just so scared, Mama. I am just so scared."

"Everyone is, honey. That's why you've got to take some risks and care for other people. To accept them for who they are and comfort them. You are too selfish in how you love people and that is why you are so scared. Life is hard for everyone, Junie. But it's kindness and compassion to others that eases the suffering of everyone. That is what really heals wounded people—kindness. It's not a sign of weakness to be a kind, loving person. It's really the root of strength. Really, Junie, you have to take another step now."

"But I'll lose myself. I know I will."

"No honey, you will deepen your understanding of who you are. It will deepen you and give you courage and faith. You've got it backwards."

I was silent on the phone with Mama for quite some time after she spoke. I love Mama Snorkel so much. I wish somebody would give her a daytime talk show and just let her sit and be Carolyn Snorkel, the nurturing woman. She is that wonderful paradox of a truly nurturing woman—strong, yet yielding when necessary; firm, yet never hammering in her delivery; honest, yet always regarding other's feelings; intuitive, yet extremely practical—no hocus pocus. And life has not been easy for her. A snakin', panty-chasin' husband, cancer, crazy kids, the

Jim and Tammy Faye bonanza, her own loneliness—and yet she remains so hopeful and loving. If I ever get rich and famous I am going to have somebody make a statue of her and stand it right next to the Lincoln Memorial or maybe in the vestibule of the Vatican, or in front of the Great Wall of China, or possibly down the road from the pyramids at Giza, or how about near that Wailing Wall in Israel? I've got to think of the perfect resting spot for her—some place with centralized air-conditioning. I must not forget this important detail.

Moments before I hung up with Mama, Daddy Snorkel picked up the phone in their bedroom. "I'm gonna be watchin' your ass, so behave yourself, goddamn it— Excuse me, Mama, I didn't know you were still on the phone. But, never you mind, Junie—I got my eye on your every move." I don't know why he hates me so much, but I swear that man never liked me. I phoned Sharon over at Roland's to apologize for being so thoughtless. Mama Snorkel is absolutely right, I have been a self-centered, ugly buzzard to good old Sharon.

"Junie, for God's sake it is two-thirty in the morning. Why are you calling over to Roland's at this hour? We're trying to get some sleep. Now what do you want?" she said, fouling the air with her intense anger for me.

"I called to apologize to you from the bottom of my heart for not being more supportive and encouraging to you and your relationship with Roland. I admire how much you have changed and I hope some day to be more like the woman you have become. It is my greatest wish to be more like you, Sharon," I philandered obsequiously.

"Oh, go fuck yourself, Junie Lake."

Click.

Well. I guess that's her way of letting me know she loves me too. Yep, she's really turned herself into a nurturing woman.

Since I had succeeded in pissing off every member of the Snorkel household I decided to call Karen to see if she was awake. I'm on a roll here and I know Steve is moving out this weekend. I wanted to check on her and see how she was feeling.

"Karen, did I wake you up?" I whispered.

"Not at all. Hey, how'd it go with Bucky-boy? Did you guys do it?"

"Nah, nothing below the belt. Sharon wants to find my face on the back of a milk carton as a missing person. She's furious that I spent the night with him. What's up with Steve?"

"Sharon's weird. Oh, I've got so much to tell you about Steve. The broad left her husband and she and Steve have gotten a place together down in the East Village. Why don't you jump in a cab and come down here. I can't sleep and I want to show you what I've been doing."

"Jesus, Karen, are you okay? That's awful . . . how'd you find out? Wait—I'll come down to your place. I'll be there in ten minutes."

"Hey, you want me to make us a salad?"

"Yeah, make a big salad. Do you want me to bring anything?"

"Bring your vegetable drawer."

Nobody in New York City bothers you when you are a woman wandering the streets wearing a quilted satin bathrobe over a pair of drop-seat pajamas lugging around a vegetable drawer. No need to bother with the can of mace. When I jumped into a cab the driver turned around and inquired, "Hey, you ain't carrying a dead animal in that thing, are ya?" I smiled back at him and said, "No sir. It's my dinner. Care for a radish?" When Karen opened the door she was chewing a large mouthful of carrot salad. "God, Junie, do you really think it's safe to be walking around the streets in your bathrobe? Here, let me help you with that," she said, taking the drawer from me.

"What's different about your apartment? This place feels different."

"I bought those flowers for the coffee table and pulled out my mother's handmade quilt from the closet. What's different is this place has some color. What did you bring?"

Steve left all of the furniture they had bought together. At first he wanted to go fifty-fifty on everything until Karen reminded him that she had paid for everything herself. Their split was civil and hollow—no teary good-bye, no last roll in the hay, no flinging of any dishes—just, "I'll see ya, Karen." After he picked up his last box, she sat on the rag rug on her bathroom floor and cried for two solid hours. For a moment she thought of killing herself, but then she realized that she is too vain to execute the desire.

"I thought of sticking my head in the oven and turning up the gas. But then I thought about the paramedics finding me with my fat ass hanging out of the oven and I could just read the headline of the *New York Post*: 'Crane needed to airlift supermodel's fat ass out of Gotham oven—exclusive photo on page 11.' I just couldn't handle the thought of that being the last high-fashion picture I ever did," Karen said, shaking her head.

The fact that Steve moved in right away with another woman was very hard on Karen, but not devastating. In many ways she has felt completely alone her entire life. She is used to picking herself up and moving on. It was nothing new for her. That empty feeling as she packed up his things and moved them into the hallway was something that felt very familiar. "I've moved so many men out of my life that I should own a packing company. I'd be richer than rich."

What was different now was how she spent her time

alone. Karen did not go back to bed and pull the drapes.
Soon after he left, the superintendent of her building
dropped off the boxes of Adriatic blue Italian tile Steve
had ordered months ago. When she opened the box
Karen noticed that a number of them had been cracked
in the shipping. Oddly enough, Karen found the chips of
vibrant azure blue flecked with sea green strokes of color
very inspiring. "I found these little chicklets of blues and
greens and ruby reds so beautiful when I scooped them
up in my hands. They were little gems of fractured beauty
. . . so unpredictable." She bought some tile grout from
the hardware store down the street and cracked the remaining tiles on her kitchen floor. One by one, Karen
stuck little flakes of Mediterranean color to the gray
Sheetrock of her kitchen walls. The blue and red and
green bursts of beauty radiated off the walls—so alive
and kinetic. It made her excited to see what she had created. At one point she ran into her bedroom and pulled
out a box of glass beads she had collected since she was
a child. Some of the beads looked like cats eyes—golden
brown and hypnotic. She added them to the cracks between the Adriatic-colored starbursts mounted on the
kitchen wall. Karen worked for hours not even noticing
Steve had gone. She just kept adding a fleck of blue here
and a bead of shimmering amber gold there. It was as if
she had been set free some place inside of herself. "I
don't know what took over me. It's as if I came alive from
the box of broken tile. I kept seeing this incredible mosaic in my mind. It was so clear the way it should go on
the wall. I felt as if something was directing my hand to
make a design that I had never seen before. I pulled fake
gems and sea pearls out of old earrings and added them
in their perfect place. It was as if some divine hand was
guiding my every movement. Let me show you what I
have done."

When Karen walked me into the kitchen I was

stunned. I had never seen anything like it before in my life. A kaleidoscope of so many swirls and drips of pulsing colors and shapes. Like a pirate's chest of precious gems all toppled and piled up on top of each other. "Jesus, this is so exquisite, Karen. I can't believe what you have done here. It's so . . ." I trailed off in amazement. She put her arms around me and gave me a big hug. "It's very clever, don't you think, Miss Junie? I'm becoming quite the clever woman, wouldn't you agree?" I hugged her as hard as I could. I was so proud of her. I don't know how she did it, but she created this mesmerizing wall of colorful, vibrating beauty. It was as if she were able to find that place deep within herself that was all prism and faceted and projected it into this positively amazing tile mosaic.

"Okay, let's not go overboard. My kitchen looks better than it did. It livens the place up a bit. Now help me wash this lettuce," she said, walking the vegetable drawer into the bathroom.

"You've got to get a kitchen sink, Karen. That's got to be next on the list."

It was very hard for me to tell Karen how incredible I thought her mosaic wall looked. Karen is very uncomfortable with compliments. They make her very nervous, as if she is calling too much attention to herself. "Enough already, it's not like I discovered another universe, Junie."

But she was wrong. She had discovered that universe within her.

The rebirth of another clever cook.

I showed Karen a little trick when we were washing the lettuce. "You should add a couple of tablespoons of salt to leech out any leftover sand and dirt, especially from the organic stuff."

Karen seemed a little confused by my suggestion. "But doesn't that really kill the notion of buying organic vegetables in the first place? To add all that salt?"

"You want to eat horse manure and fish eyeballs and cow dung in your salad, Karen? 'Cause that's what they use to fertilize this stuff. Haven't you eaten enough shit in your life? Do you really need a salad of it?" I said, putting my hand on my hip.

"Get the salt."

I was grateful that Karen didn't feel the need to get into a philosophical debate about this organic lettuce thing. Cleaning exotic lettuce is usually more difficult than the rather pedestrian iceberg lettuce. Sandy leaves like arugula, escarole, curly endive and watercress are best left soaking for a few minutes in salted water, then dried individually on sheets of paper towels. You have to be very thorough with delicate lettuce and be very careful to not only wash the leaves completely, but to gently pat them dry so you won't have a soggy bowl of salad. Another good idea is to lightly steam hard-to-digest vegetables such as broccoli, cauliflower and carrots before adding them to your salad. Steaming these vegetables intensifies their natural color and flavor. But frankly my friends, Karen and I won't be adding any hard-to-digest vegetables to our salad bowl. "Here—put some potato salad in the corner and add more croutons. Do you want me to fry up some Canadian bacon? Why do you have so many carrots and celery in your vegetable drawer? Didn't you bring any walnuts and raisins with you?" Karen said, looking as if I had run over her dog.

"They're down in the bottom of the drawer, just keep looking. Do you have any olives I can add to this thing? Or how about some Cheetos? They taste great in a salad, better than croutons," I suggested.

What is so great about salads is that you can add absolutely anything to them and they'll still taste wonderful. Obviously, Karen and I use the excuse of salad making to blow our lifelong diets. Most women are far more health conscious when making salads. I don't really know what to say about that, other than to tell you to get another cookbook if you're looking for organic recipes. Maybe Holly will do a cookbook and you can buy hers. If we were in my kitchen I'd shave some fresh Parmesan onto the salad. Wait a minute. . . . No I wouldn't. I don't have any fresh Parmesan in my refrigerator, so I don't know what I am talking about here. I was on the verge of lying to you and I apologize. It's because I haven't slept.

Karen made a *fab-u-lous* cilantro lime dressing that added the perfect zing to our garden-fresh monstrosity. I reminded her of the time we made a lamb salad with roasted garlic, new potatoes and green beans. It was stupendous. Karen once made a wicked batch of cold Chinese sesame noodles, which makes for an unusual cold pasta salad—very *kung fu-ab-u-lous*. Between the two of us, Karen and I must have a hundred salad recipes. I have a mind-boggling wild rice and chicken salad that goes great as a main course when entertaining. Karen has a terrific steak and artichoke heart salad that is delicious when served warm over a bed of peppery arugula leaves. She also serves it with the best loaf of Parmesan garlic bread that I have ever tasted. I know it has nothing to do with salads but I'm adding the bread to this chapter because it's too delicious. You can also ask anyone in this town who makes the best tarragon-walnut chicken salad and they'll say Junie Bell Lake. I'm like the Larry King of chicken salad.

Karen and I loaded up two serving platters of salad. I added a few slivers of carrot and celery for a nice refreshing crunch in between scoops of potato salad, carrot salad, tabouli salad and Cheetos. Karen handed me six Oreo cookies as we left the kitchen. "Here, carry these so we won't have to make another trip. God forbid we burn any calories tonight," she said.

It must have been around five thirty in the morning

when we sat down on the floor of her living room. Karen handed me a can of Coca-Cola hanging from the pocket of one of Steve's white T-shirts." I grabbed this for you." Daylight was just creeping out from behind the giant gray spiral of the Chrysler building. First time in weeks it looked like it wasn't going to rain, more like a lazy winter sun with lots of glow, but little actual heat. I'll probably need to borrow a coat when I finally leave.

"So, are you gonna be all right Karen?" I asked, setting the plate on her glass coffee table.

"I've been through worse than this. I'll be okay, I think. That's the trouble with being a survivor though, you learn to survive anything that comes your way," Karen answered very matter-of-factly.

"Yeah, surviving becomes second nature after a while. It's learning how to just live that's so difficult. I remember once when I was about twenty-six, I ran to the emergency room at New York Hospital because I thought I was having a heart attack—my heart was pounding, my head felt like it was going to explode, I couldn't breathe. It was awful, really awful. A doctor hooked me up to all of these monitors and studied the results as they beeped into the palm of his hands. He looked up at me and said, 'I've got horrible news for you. You've had another panic attack. I guess a real bad one. So, you are going to live and you are going to have to find a way to deal with that fact.' Later he asked me if I wanted a prescription for Valium and I told him I didn't take pills anymore. He looked up from my chart and said, 'Well, then I guess you're going to have to do it on your own,' and he left the room without saying good-bye."

"Yeah, but Junie, you're not that same girl anymore," Karen said, taking a sip from my Coca-Cola.

"You're right, Karen. I'm not starving to death for someone to love me."

"I know what you mean. I feel exactly the same way.

We've begun to feed that place between our hearts and our stomachs. It makes life so much easier to accept."

I crawled onto Karen's white overstuffed couch after I had finished eating my salad. Karen threw her mother's handmade quilt over me and carried the plates into the kitchen. The last thing I thought about as I put my head down on the pillow was that I was glad that I never succeeded in killing myself. I tried to a lot, you know. I'd crawl in bed and take a fistful of pills and slowly drift away. Sometimes I'd drift for days, sometimes for weeks—just drifting toward someplace where I could feel safe. "See if you can get some sleep, Junie. You probably didn't get too much this weekend," she said, patting my head.

"I'll help you with the dishes later," I said, starting to doze off. "What are you going to do?"

"I'm going back to my wall. I've got something I want to try . . . a new design. I'll see ya when you wake up. Get some sleep now, everything is okay today," she whispered lightly.

Life is good.
    Thank you God for another day.
    And for helping Karen.
    —JUNIE

Karen's Fresh Pineapple and Carrot Salad

SERVES 2

1 cup fresh pineapple,
    peeled, cored and
    cubed
1 cup peeled and grated
    carrots

1 stalk celery, thinly
    sliced
2 tablespoons scallions
    (optional)
Dressing (recipe follows)

Combine all the ingredients in a serving bowl. Add the desired amount of dressing and toss to combine. Serve cold.

Dressing

MAKES 1 CUP

½ cup corn oil
2 tablespoons rice wine
    vinegar
1 teaspoon soy sauce

¼ teaspoon salt
1 teaspoon sugar
1 clove garlic, minced

Put all the ingredients in a jar, cover and shake until well mixed or blend in food processor.

Lamb Salad with Roasted Garlic and New Potatoes

SERVES 2 TO 3

2 cups leftover cooked
   lamb, cubed
1 whole head of garlic,
   roasted (see Note)
½ pound green beans,
   steamed
½ cup feta cheese
2 tablespoons fresh mint

2 tablespoons dill
½ red onion, thinly sliced
½ cup pitted black olives,
   sliced lengthwise
10 to 12 new potatoes,
   unpeeled, halved
Balsamic vinaigrette (recipe follows)

Preheat the oven to 350 degrees. In a large mixing bowl toss together the lamb, garlic, green beans, feta cheese, mint, dill, red onion and black olives. Cover and refrigerate.

In a large pot, bring 4 quarts of water to a boil. Add the potatoes and boil until tender, about 12 minutes. Allow to cool, and add to salad. Add the vinaigrette and toss to combine. Cover and return bowl to refrigerator and marinate for at least 3 hours before serving.

Note: To roast garlic, separate but do not peel the cloves. Place them in a small baking dish and brush with olive oil. Roast for one hour in a 350-degree oven, or until golden. Allow to cool and peel the skins.

Balsamic Vinaigrette

MAKES 1¾ CUPS

½ cup balsamic vinegar
1 cup olive oil
2 cloves garlic, minced
1 tablespoon Dijon
    mustard

1 teaspoon sugar
Salt and pepper to taste

Put all the ingredients in a jar, cover and shake well or blend in a food processor.

Note: This is a great salad for leftover lamb, but is one big pain in the ass to make from scratch. It's a great recipe when used as a solution to leftover food, so you can substitute steak, veal or chicken for the lamb.

San Francisco Spicy Chinese Chicken Salad

SERVES 5

5 cups cooked chicken
    meat or ½ roasting
    chicken
1 pound spaghetti
2 bunches scallions,
    washed and chopped
1 4-ounce can water
    chestnuts, drained
    and thinly sliced
1 bunch fresh cilantro,
    chopped

Soy dressing (recipe
    follows)
1 small head iceberg let-
    tuce, washed and
    shredded
1 cup roasted peanuts,
    crushed
1 medium cucumber,
    peeled, seeded and
    thinly sliced

Remove skin and bones from the chicken and tear into shreds and set aside.

Cook spaghetti according to package instructions, drain and combine with the chicken, scallions, water chestnuts and cilantro. Add the dressing and combine. Refrigerate for at least 3 hours before serving.

To serve, arrange the lettuce on a serving platter and top with the salad. Garnish with the peanuts and cucumber.

Soy Dressing

¼ cup corn oil
¼ cup sesame oil
¼ cup rice wine vinegar
1 tablespoon fresh lemon
    juice
1 tablespoon soy sauce
1 tablespoon grated
    ginger

2 large cloves garlic,
    minced
¼ teaspoon hot pepper
    flakes
1 tablespoon sugar
4 tablespoons chunky
    peanut butter

Place all the ingredients in a food processor or blender
and process until thoroughly emulsified (turns white).

Pork Tenderloin and Wild Rice Salad

SERVES 6 TO 8

½ cup raisins
⅔ cup dried apricots, cut
　　into pieces
1 cup dry sherry
2 pounds pork tenderloin
4 tablespoons apricot jam
1 cup ginger ale
1 cup slivered almonds
2 6-ounce boxes long-
　　grain and wild rice

2 stalks celery, chopped
½ cup scallions, thinly
　　sliced
½ cup fresh parsley,
　　chopped
1 cup Balsamic Vinai-
　　grette (see page 217)
1 bunch fresh watercress,
　　washed and trimmed

Preheat the oven to 350 degrees.

Soak the raisins and apricots in the dry sherry for 2 to 3 minutes to soften.

Place the pork in a greased roasting pan, coat with the apricot jam, then pour the ginger ale over top and roast for about 2 hours. At the same time place the almonds on a cookie sheet and toast in the oven until golden brown, 4 to 6 minutes, stirring occasionally so as not to burn.

Cook the rice according to package instructions and allow to cool. In a large bowl, combine the rice, raisins, apricots, celery, scallions, parsley and toasted almonds. Pour in the Balsamic Vinaigrette and toss.

On a large serving plate make a bed of the watercress and arrange the wild-rice salad on top. After the pork tenderloin has cooled, slice it into thin medallions and arrange on the salad. Serve cold.

Steak and Artichoke Heart Salad

SERVES 4

4 8-ounce fillet mignons,
  each 2 inches thick
2 6-ounce jars of mari-
  nated artichoke
  hearts
1 medium red onion,
  thinly sliced
2 stalks celery, thinly
  sliced
1 bunch fresh basil,
  chopped

1 bunch flat-leaf Italian
  parsley, chopped
1 teaspoon ground black
  pepper
1 bunch arugula
1 head Bibb lettuce
1 cup Balsamic Vinai-
  grette (see page 217)

Preheat the broiler. Arrange fillets on a foil-lined broiler
plate and broil 2 to 3 inches away from the flame for
3 to 4 minutes on each side for medium-rare steaks. Remove, cool and cut into ½-inch strips. Place the strips
into a mixing bowl and add the artichoke hearts and the
liquid, the red onion, celery, basil, parsley, pepper and
dressing. Toss to combine and place on a bed of arugula
and Bibb lettuce. Serve cold with extra vinaigrette on the
side.

Garlic Parmesan Cheese Loaf

SERVES 4 TO 6

½ cup olive oil
2 cloves garlic, minced
4 tablespoons chopped
fresh basil
2 tablespoons chopped
fresh parsley

⅓ cup Parmesan cheese
1 loaf crusty French or
Italian bread, halved
lengthwise

Preheat the oven to 400 degrees. Combine all the ingredients, except the bread, in a small mixing bowl and spread onto the cut sides of the bread. Place the halves on a cookie sheet cut side up and bake for 10 to 12 minutes, or until bubbly.

Tarragon-Walnut Chicken Salad

SERVES 3

2 boneless chicken
   breasts, split
2 stalks celery, thinly
   sliced
1 bunch scallions,
   chopped
½ cup walnuts, coarsely
   chopped

1 tablespoon chopped
   fresh tarragon
½ cup sour cream
4 tablespoons mayonnaise
1 tablespoon lemon juice
1 tablespoon olive oil
½ cup walnuts
1 bunch watercress

Bring 3 quarts of water with a little olive oil to a boil. Add the chicken and cook for 8 to 10 minutes, or until white and firm. Drain and set aside to cool.

In a large mixing bowl combine the sour cream, mayonnaise, lemon juice and tarragon. Add the celery and scallion and blend well.

Cut the chicken into bite-size pieces, add to the sour cream mixture and toss. Cover and refrigerate. Just before serving, line a platter with the watercress, garnish with walnuts and serve.

BASIC KITCHEN EQUIPMENT

Toaster oven
Can opener
Paper towel rack
Corkscrew
Mesh-lined strainer
Potato peeler
Soup ladle
Measuring cups
Measuring spoons
Metal spatula
Rubber spatula
Rectangular cake pans
    (2)
Round cake pans (2)
Nonstick baking sheet
Loaf pan
Paring knife
Cook's knife, 6 inches
    long

Chef's knife, 8 inches
    long
Carving knife, 10
    inches long
Serrated bread knife
Garlic press
Wooden spoons
Bottle opener
Salad spinner
Drip coffee pot
Tea kettle
Salt and pepper
    shakers
Wire whisk
Kitchen scissors
Mixing bowls—4 sizes
Hand-held grater

POTS AND PANS

2-quart saucepan
8- to 10-quart
    saucepan
10-inch frying pan
2- to 3-quart casserole

Roasting pan with
    wire rack
Vegetable steamer
Colander

BASIC SPICE RACK

Basil
Chili powder
Curry powder
Ground ginger
Ground nutmeg
Paprika, sweet
Black pepper
White pepper
Kosher salt
Rosemary
Sweet basil

Cinnamon
Dill weed
Dried mint leaves
Oregano
Ground sage
Cilantro
Chili pepper flakes
Thyme
Tarragon leaves
Cumin

BASIC CLEANING PRODUCTS

Liquid dish soap
Dishwasher soap
White vinegar
Ammonia
Powdered cleanser
Bleach
Sponges

Brillo pads
Windex
Silver cleaner
Paper towels
Scrub brush
Cotton kitchen towels
Oven mitts (2)

As the World Churns

So Roland finally goosed Sharon.

Crudely put, but nonetheless accurately reported. How I got wind of this information was through Evie. It seems Sharon called her to find the name of a reputable gynecologist in response to yet another ugly flare-up of cystitis—the honeymooners' love sting. Maybe now that she has gotten a little S.E.X., she'll shape the hell up and police that vile mouth of hers.

"Oh, grow up, Junie, and just be happy for her. Sharon said it was the most emotional sexual experience she has ever had. He even went to the doctor with her to make sure she was going to be all right. Sounds like a great guy," Evie said.

"Most emotional experience—right. She said that about Spooky too. How'd she get your phone number?"

"Oh, we talked for a while the other day when I called over to your place looking for you. I gave it to her in case she needed anything. She's a great girl, Junie—cut her some slack."

Evie's independent thinking is one personality trait that I really despise. "What? I'm supposed to agree with everything you say?"

Well, it would be nice for a change.

"No one else gets to go through any period of adjustment but you. Is that what you are trying to tell me?"

Yes, that is what I am trying to convey to her.

"Well, then you're an asshole."

Why, thank you, Evie.

The first time Sharon and Roland made love was the night after their cocktail party. That night was very special for Sharon. For the first time she felt she was an equal partner with Roland. He needed her in a way that allowed her to feel competent and respected. Sharon planned the guest list, sent out the invitations—using her steady calligraphic hand to address each envelope—and ordered the flower arrangements to be delivered in the late afternoon. Roland was very worried that people would not come to his cocktail party. He doesn't really have a flair for people and he is smart enough to know this about himself. Sharon made sure to add a special little request on each invitation to let guests know how much it would mean to Roland if they would come. Each note was carefully thought out before it was written. Not pandering and insincere, but thoughtful and sensitive in a way Sharon felt best reflected Roland's professional image.

Roland was deeply touched by Sharon's sensitivity and style when dealing with his colleagues. Her presence made him feel less nervous and apprehensive about socializing with the movers and shakers in this town. He was growing to depend on her in ways that he never before had been able to with a woman. He trusted she

MS. SHARON SNORKEL LOVIT

Dear Judge Rheinbeck,

It meant so much to Roland that you invited him to the dinner in your honor the other evening. He told me later that night about how kind you were to him when he was starting his practice. Things like that are not forgotten by Roland and I know he would be so touched if you would come to his home and share in some good wine and conversation.

Look forward to seeing you Friday night.

> *Respectfully,*
> *Sharon Snorkel Lovit*

would never reveal to the outside world how little he really thought of himself. Sharon's love and tenderness made him feel his own dignity. It gave him courage to set bigger goals for his future.

Roland also depended on her to organize the party so that coats would be taken from guests as they arrived and people were not left standing at the door with no one to greet them and make them feel welcome. Sharon covered all the bases in a way that looked effortless and graceful. He admired her ability to remember important details about people's personal lives. "Oh Dr. Mayhan, have you finished building your harpsichord yet? You must let Roland and I come see it when you have. Let me take your coat. . . ." Roland forgot that Dr. Mayhan was building a harpsichord, what a relief to him Sharon had remembered.

When the party was over, Roland asked Sharon to sit next to him on the couch in the living room. He was anxious to hear what she thought about the people she had met that evening. "I'll be there in a minute, honey.

Roland, make sure to give the coat-check girl a nice tip and thank her for all she did this evening." When she said this to him, Roland rubbed his eyes and laughed silently to himself. He would have let the girl go home without a tip or a thank you. Sharon understood the political value of remembering personal details—a matter of pivotal importance in his line of work.

When they were finally alone Roland kissed Sharon in a way that he never had before. She was a little surprised by his newfound passion for her. Prior to this, their kisses had only been distant with a hint of gentleness— no real spark of communion. It worried her a bit that the relationship might eventually wind up friendly and respectful, but empty of any true erotic zip. But this was no longer the case between the two of them. He was limber and sensual as he stroked her body with his loving hands. Roland had put on an old Tony Bennett tape and the two of them rocked slowly to the low sways and high hums of the music while all alone with the lights off. He held her in a way that conveyed he wanted and adored her for the woman she had become. She was so grateful that this moment between them had finally arrived. Mama Snorkel had promised her that if she waited and let a man really know her, she would feel loved in a way that Sharon had never felt before.

The two of them swayed slowly into the bedroom, letting each lingering kiss guide them closer toward the bed. They spoke softly with each other about the need for condoms and if Sharon had proper birth control. This small conversation brought up a wellspring of feelings in Sharon. It made her think about the baby she had given up. It made her think about the consequences of loving a man who didn't respond with the same regard to what was important to her.

The memory of all of this made her cry as Roland started to undress her. She was starting to get angry that

he didn't ask her what she was crying about. His silence
scared her that he might have grown use to ignoring a
woman's tears. She pulled his hand off of her breast for
a moment and told him to pay attention to the fact she
was crying. Roland was at a loss for words—but Sharon
was not. She told him that if they were going to make
love, certain commitments between the two of them
would have to be agreed upon. Namely, an AIDS test and
a detailed history of his previous sexual encounters. He
agreed. Secondly, she would need to know what his in-
tentions were for their future together. Was he serious?
And if so, how serious?—"More details, please." Roland
said he was very serious and asked Sharon if she would
consider moving to New York to be closer to him. Was
this a proposal of marriage? Is that what he was stating
to her with his pants unzipped? No, not exactly, but a
serious, very serious analysis of their impending future.
Sharon was not pleased with his answer. It lacked specific
details and commitments.

Against her better instincts she made love with him.
The tone between the two of them was loving, but Sharon's mind kept slipping into a worried concentration as
he laid on top of her penetrating her empty womb. She
feared that she might regret this as soon as it was over.
Roland whispered that he had never loved anyone as passionately as he had Sharon. She didn't know what this
really meant, but kissed him deeply as he spoke. She
reminded herself that love takes time to trust and feel
comfortable. "Love takes time," she repeated over and
over to herself.

Sharon rocked Roland to sleep and later, after she
was certain he was sound asleep, she slipped out from
under the sheets to call her mother. Sharon dragged the
phone into the bathroom and locked the door behind
her. Mama told her not to worry and that she had done
the best she could given all the fear she was up against

inside of herself. She asked Mama if she would ever be able to really feel loved by a man. Mama said she felt that it had happened between the two of them that night and now it was up to Sharon to trust that she was worth loving. This type of trust did not come easily to Sharon. It, too, would take some time.

"Sharon is joining you, me and Karen for dinner tonight so get comfortable with the idea or just go home," Evie commanded as we walked into her bedroom.

"I'll be nice, but I'm warning you, she's gonna be a total downer. A monolithic bummer in Pendleton wool slacks. You watch, Evie."

"Nah, she won't. She'll be a little cool to you, but she's not gonna make a scene. Sharon's not the type. Besides she knows you are going to be here—so she must be ready for some kind of truce."

"What's she bringing for dinner?"

"Dessert," Evie answered.

"Oh great, she'll bring chocolate-covered banana cream goo. She only makes desserts that have bananas and that taste like shit."

"I'm warning you. If you start any trouble, I'm throwing your ass out of here. I don't want any more stress."

Evie and I had this conversation while we were cleaning out her walk-in closet, which was about to be transformed into the baby's room. "The construction guys are coming on Thursday and this place has got to be totally cleaned out. Let me know if there are any old clothes that you want." Evie has the best apartment in New York City. From every window there is a panoramic view of Central Park. Even the closet has a little church window that looks directly out onto the West Seventy-second Street entrance.

"The baby's room is going to be a soft, cozy butter yellow and will lead straight into our bathroom—that way we can have her changing room and bedroom all in one place. Good idea, don't you think?" she said, stuffing a pair of gold lamé cocktail slippers into a cardboard box.

"You said *her* as if you know the baby is a girl—do you know something?" I asked, deciding whether I wanted to take her old mink coat.

"I know it's a girl. It's just something I sense so strongly. Don't wear that mink on Fifty-seventh Street, those animal rights people hang out around there and will harass you unmercifully if you do. Only wear it on Park or Fifth and nobody will give you any shit."

Sol took Lucky to visit his mother in Brooklyn Heights so we could begin transforming Evie's over-size closet into a safe harbor for their baby. Which was hard to imagine as I looked at hanger after hanger of expensive silk labels and assorted sizes and shapes of leather handbags dangling from metal hooks, and a steady stream of chiffon scarves and cashmere sweaters spilling out from every corner. "It's amazing you can even get dressed in the morning. How can you find anything in here?" I said, rummaging through her luxurious remains.

"I can't, so I go out and buy another color until I run into the original again," she said laughing.

I sat on the floor of her closet while Evie handed me the castaways from her life as a single woman. "Size eight, can you believe I ever fit into a size eight? This must be from my drug days. Here, see if you can fit into it. It's a St. Laurent jumpsuit. I paid a fortune for it," she said, accidently dropping it on my head.

I was being swallowed up by layers and layers of exotic fabric. I started to yank clothes out of drawers that had been jammed on top of each other. Cotton halter tops mixed in with Chanel cardigans that had been crammed underneath suede riding pants. "Hey, when did you ever go riding? I mean, why do you have a pair of suede riding pants?" I asked, holding them up to see if they would fit me.

"Oh, I think they're from an affair I had with a guy who was into polo. I think I wore them to a polo match out in the Hamptons. But then I saw a picture of myself wearing them and I looked like I had phone books growing out of the tops of my thighs. I never wore them again. Don't take those, they'll make you look worse than the horse you are riding. Just put them in the Goodwill box," she said, pulling down a box of hair ribbons and headbands from the top shelf.

Evie's life was changing in ways that were making her worry about her career as a commodities trader. The pressure and constant battling for position and profit also worried her about the health of the baby. "It's too much for me. Maybe another type of woman can handle it, but I can't do everything right now. I'm not balancing the extremes in my life very well." But the thought of resigning from a position she had fought so hard to get was not the answer to her problem. "Hey, I'm a tough broad. I love what I do and I don't want to just walk away from it all. I've worked too hard. But look, it's the type of dog-eat-dog business where your reputation is only as good as what your numbers are at the end of the day. It's a daily struggle for respect but I love it. And I'm good at what I do," she stated, as she carried an armful of business suits into the bedroom.

"So what are you going to do?" I asked, trying on a silver mesh baseball cap.

"I think I am going to take an early maternity leave, which is really gonna fuck me up professionally, but I really need to get my life organized to be a mother. You know, I've got to learn what it feels like to be around the house during the day. I've never been the type of person to hang around my house, so I've got to develop some hobbies and get into this or I am going to be a nervous wreck. I definitely want to work after the baby is born, but I've got to set up my life so that I know everything is being taken care of. This is gonna really hurt me. The guys at the office already treat me differently now that I am pregnant. They don't tell me dirty jokes or scream orders at me anymore. When they scream at you, it's their way of letting you know that you have earned their respect, that they feel comfortable with you. But, that's all changed," she said, dumping the suits on her bed.

Evie likes the power and demands of her career. The qualities it takes for a woman to effectively swim in the middle of a shark tank are innate within Evie's being. She's a master at negotiating deals and cutting right into the power structure of a trading floor. She fought hard to compete in this macho business and she has stepped on a lot of toes. "I know there are people I work with who are thrilled I am pregnant because they see it as the demise of my authority in that office and that bugs the hell out of me. I don't like what this pregnancy is doing to my power base. People don't revere me with the same terror they once did when I walk in the front door."

Evie is trying to cleverly balance her life as a business barracuda with being a loving mother—not an easy thing, no matter how much power and money a woman acquires. "Pregnancy is seen as a weakness and people use it against you. They see you as a wounded competitor in the deal, not on equal footing, so they start to box in a different ring." At this stage in her career, Evie finds it hard to make the compromises in her professional life. "I can certainly work at home, but it isolates me from what's going on down at work . . . but I may have to temporarily accept that right now. Sol and I have agreed I would go back to work right after the baby is born. He's in a different place in his life. He doesn't want to get back into the jungle. And that is just fine with me. I know I'd go crazy if I gave up my career forever. But this interim problem of having to take time off for the baby is not a natural thing for me. It's taking the spin off my ball."

Evie and I came to the profound conclusion that the only time life is really in cosmic balance with the universe is when you are dead and buried. "Balance equals death in my book. When your life is in perfect order it's time to check your pulse," she yelled from the back of her closet. "Oh, my God, look. There's another window in here. How great."

"You guys are right on about that," Karen said, peering into the closet.

"God, you scared me to death. I forgot you were here," I jumped, grabbing her hand. "Where have you been?"

"I fell asleep on the floor behind Evie's couch. I was trying to get more inspiration about the baby's mosaic, but I snoozed instead," Karen said, rubbing the sleep from her eyes.

Evie was so impressed with what Karen had done with her kitchen that she hired her to do a tile mosaic in the baby's bathroom. "You are not going to pay me for doing a mosaic for the baby. I wouldn't think of it, Evie," Karen said, shaking her head. Evie wouldn't let Karen come to her apartment until they had agreed that Karen would be paid for her work. "Karen, a woman should always be acknowledged for the work that comes from her inspiration. How else are you going to have a career that you love? If you are smart about this and use the visibility of your modeling career to market yourself, this could be your next step."

Tears welled up in Karen's eyes when Evie insisted on paying her. "You think it's good enough for me to do as a career? I don't have to do something that makes me feel like a worthless piece of shit to support myself?"

"No, Karen. You have been given the good fortune of growing into a woman. And your womanhood is where you create from, so just know that the older you become, the more you will have to offer. Don't ever forget that, no matter what the fuck the world tells you. So when can you start?"

Karen's thoughts were a flurry of inspiration and bloodcurdling terror. She was thrilled at the thought of doing another mosaic, but fretted that her talent and eye for shape and color was simply a momentary breath of creative madness. "Just get in there and do it, honey. You'll figure it all out—I know you will," Evie encouraged.

Karen joined us on the floor of the closet. On her hands and knees she poked her way around Evie's jewelry drawer. She found a small lacquer charm bracelet that Evie had worn as a young girl. "May I use this?" Karen queried. She continued her artistic excavation until she found more little trinkets from Evie's own childhood—a lace hair bow, a red plastic purse, a pair of tap shoes, a headless Barbie doll wearing a blue sequined prom dress. "I think I can use bits and pieces of each of these. Will you ask Sol if I can go through some of his childhood things for some more ideas?"

By the time Sharon arrived the closet was picked bone clean from the remains of Evie's former life as a single woman living on her own. "Don't put it like that. Just say that I'm putting my shit in storage until after the baby's born, Junie. God, you're making it sound like I'm giving up my identity as a woman."

Well, we're witnessing a major turning point from business woman to business mother, so I've got to jazz it up a bit.

"Why don't you start on the lasagna and let Karen and me finish up in here," Evie said as she returned from greeting Sharon at the door. "Behave yourself, I'm warning you."

"Why do I have to make the goddamn lasagna?" I said, stamping my foot on the carpet.

"*Because you're the one writing the goddamn book*

about cooking and women. And you haven't cooked in the past two chapters. Now get in there and cook!" Evie yelled.

Oh yeah. I almost forgot. Forgive me.

I found Sharon unpacking her shopping bag of sugary, plastic crap for our dessert. Trying to ignite a conversation with her was like trying to talk to a piece of sushi—a little cold and undercooked. She looked like a henna-brown version of Phyllis George in her gingham blue-checked pantsuit with corresponding blue espadrilles. "Hi, Missy Sharon. It's nice to see you at *my friend's house for dinner,"* I said, opening the refrigerator.

"I apologize, but only for what I said to you on the telephone. I still think it's a slutty thing to bed my baby brother."

"Well, Sharon, then I'm in good company because you have done plenty of slutty things over the years. Need we go back in history?"

"That won't be necessary. I'm sure that you haven't been home to see what Bucky has sent you. It was in front of your door when I went home to change this afternoon."

My heart sank into my stomach when she told me that Bucky had sent me something. I immediately thought it was bad news—like a letter attached to a human skull telling me to drop dead. I've had intense waves of guilt for being such a scum bag to him when he was still a virgin. "What is it, Sharon? What did Bucky send me?"

Sharon set a bunch of ripened bananas on the counter and folded her arms across her chest. "How should I know, I set it on the dining-room table."

Sharon is lying to me. I can tell by the squeak in her voice. "Just tell me what it is. I know you opened it, so just tell me."

I knew she knew that I knew (it gets confusing but

stay with me) that she had looked in the box. Sharon and I are psychically cabled together that way—like two big extrasensory satellite dishes. I know what she knows even when she pretends not to know what I know. She can run, but she cannot hide from me—and she knows that I know that too. "He sent you two white gardenias surrounded by a soft hollow of sea moss. He's trying to show you how much he cares about you, Junie. I would be touched if someone as dear as Bucky sent me flowers. I hope you appreciate what he's done."

"And what did the card say? . . . Don't give me the runaround, just tell me what it said," I demanded, putting my hand on my hip.

"It said something like: 'I sent these to you so you wouldn't worry about Angela—can't wait to see you, Bucky.' "

"Did he say 'love Bucky' or just 'Bucky'?" I quizzed.

"I can't remember."

Bitch. . . . Selfish bitch. Can too remember . . . she just wants to see me beg and squirm. She knows that I know that. And what's this shit about Angela? I wasn't thinking about her in the first place. Why did he have to mention her lousy name on my love card. He's ruined everything by including her name. Why is he mentioning her if he isn't seeing her? What's the fucking point? He's blown it big this time.

"Oh, stop being such a picky, thankless cow," Sharon said, reading my mind.

"Evie wants you to make the lasagna, Sharon. She's busy," I said, leaving the room.

Now am I a clever cook or what? Why, I have gotten to be so clever that I get other people to cook for me while I take all the credit. You got to hand it to me— that's clever on the verge of sheer brilliance!

I grabbed Evie's cellular phone from her briefcase

and walked out onto the terrace to call in to my answering machine. Bucky had left two incredibly romantic messages:

Message #1: "Junie, it's Bucky. . . . Call me after midnight." Click.

Message #2: "Where the hell are ya? Call me, damn it." Click.

What a manifestation of male sensitivity and tenderness and unadulterated masculine charm. Where's my vibrator at moments like these?

I reached Bucky as he was just getting out of the shower. He sounded a little harassed when he answered the phone.

"Yeah?"

"Bucky, you are the sweetest man to walk the face of the earth. I just called to tell you that. How are you doing?" I chirped, while staring off into the view of the dusky city steeple tops and neon signs.

"Oh, great, you got 'em. Mama told me what to get. So, you really like 'em, Junie?"

"They are so beautiful, Bucky. They are almost as beautiful as you are," I mushed into the receiver.

"Ah, that's great. I'm really happy you like them. I can't wait to see your big kitty cat face."

Just as I was orbiting out into the international love galaxy Evie threw open the terrace doors and poked me in the kidneys. "I can't fucking believe you—telling Sharon to make the lasagna. She's already making dessert. Now get in there and cook, damn it," she snarled, slamming the doors behind her. Bucky and I had to keep our love coos to a bare minimum, so I could run back in the kitchen and finish the lasagna.

Bummer.

"So Evie wants me to make the lasagna, huh?"

"Oh, you're not above lying, Sharon."

"I take it Bucky is doing well?" she said, handing me an onion.

"Bucky is absolutely *fab-u-lous* in every way, Sharon."

"Don't press your luck, honey."

I called a momentary truce by showing Sharon how to make a scrumptious white artichoke lasagna that I had made up from my own vivid imagination. She was definitely impressed as she watched me mix the ricotta cheese in with some Parmesan and add a tiny pinch of dried mint to lighten the rich, cheesy taste of the dish. Fresh mint in lasagna—even when making the traditional kind with tomato sauce—adds a wonderful fresh flavor. It also helps to incorporate the wide variety of spices and herbs that are used in any recipe. Sharon's enthusiasm for the dish enabled her to be kind enough to boil the noodles. I quickly layered the noodles, the cheese mixture, the sautéed artichoke hearts, mushrooms and onions and then a layer of grated mozzarella cheese. The white artichoke lasagna tastes best when it is made a day ahead of time, but still tastes great when you make it the same day.

God love Karen, but her sautéed zucchini and tomato slop was ceremoniously dropped from the night's menu. "What's wrong with this? Why does it taste so acidic?" she pouted. Sharon explained to her that sometimes cooking stewed tomatoes in a metal saucepan can give them an incredibly tart aftertaste. "It's not your fault, angel. It happens sometimes. Why don't we steam up some of these green beans instead," Sharon said, patting Karen on the back.

Karen turned to me and whispered, "Do we hate her or have we forgiven her?"

Making sure that Sharon couldn't hear us, I mouthed the words, "It's still touch and go."

"I gotcha," Karen nodded.

"I gotcha too, Junie," Sharon said as she slapped the bag of green beans into my hands. "Why don't you clean these while Karen and I go relax in the living room?"

While I was left to finish cooking dinner, Sharon and Karen flipped on the news and relaxed with a couple of glasses of white wine. No one bothered to turn off the stereo, which was softly playing Brazilian jazz in the background. Nobody was paying attention to either, but nobody wanted to do anything about all the distraction. Evie flew into the kitchen and dumped a wedge of Brie onto a serving plate with some Triscuits. "Please. Don't give me any flak about serving cheese and crackers. Everything is too disorganized for me to even think up anything very creative." She flew out.

If Evie would have stayed in the kitchen I would have told her it was a very clever idea to serve cheese and crackers. I think it's very clever of her to realize that everything is too overwhelming for her to be worrying about impressing people and pushing herself beyond her natural limit. She respects herself enough to know she doesn't have to do it all perfectly. She doesn't tear herself to shreds for not having the perfect appetizers. Instead, she's out in her living room relaxing and enjoying her friends.

I flopped on the couch next to Evie and asked Sharon to pass me the Brie. We sat around in a semi-circle and discussed monumentally important topics of the day. "Peter Jennings is one giant hunk of burnin' love, wouldn't you agree, ladies?" Sharon said, toasting him on the television with her wine glass. With mouths stuffed full, the entire room nodded in agreement.

Evie jumped up from the couch in a burst of energy. "Let's eat out on the terrace tonight. Wouldn't that be fun, you guys?" This was a very unclever idea if you ask me and I wasn't afraid to assert myself. "For Christ's sake, it's got to be thirty degrees out there tonight. We'll freeze to death."

"No you won't because I'll give everyone a coat, a blanket and some wool socks and you will all be toasty warm. Sol and I do this all the time. Look . . . look and see how clear and beautiful it is out there."

Everyone else seemed game to eat dinner out on the terrace. Sharon helped Evie set the table while Karen and I finished fixing dinner. Karen sliced some succulent fresh cantaloupe and pineapple to serve alongside the white artichoke lasagna and sautéed green beans. When I pulled the bubbling hot lasagna out of the oven, Karen sautéed the green beans in olive oil and lemon until they were crispy-tender. "Are you guys ready to sit down and eat?" I hollered out toward the terrace.

"Yep, let me just grab the coats and blankets," Evie yelled back.

One by one we dressed in the hallway to compete with the blistering elements. I wore Evie's floor-length sable coat inside out with a red woolen ski mask and pink sweat socks. I gave my wool blanket to Karen, who was zipping up her black hooded ski parka with simulated fake fur. "I wonder if she has any mittens," she asked while pulling on a pair of powder blue cashmere socks.

Evie had thrown on one of Sol's ski sweaters underneath his stitched black leather trench coat. "Don't worry, it's lined with rabbit fur, I think," she said as she bent over to pull on a pair of wool booties.

"Why, I've never had so much fun," Sharon squealed as she wrapped a plaid car blanket around Evie's camel hair coat.

"Here Sharon, put this fur turban on your head. I

have no idea why I bought that ugly thing," Evie said, looking confused.

Swaddled together looking like a small bus load of well-dressed Russian peasants, the four of us dined over the canyons of city lights flickering in the distance. Evie's silver candelabra added an elegant glow to the meal as we shivered and reached for the passing plates in the crisp winter night. I had never seen Karen look so beautiful as she did buried underneath her hood of fake fur. It was the first time in years I had heard her really, really laugh from her guts. She looked happy, really happy, and her face wore a peaceful, yet exuberant expression. I had never seen a picture of her like that—at peace with herself, in her own body, laughing. It was so nice to see.

Sharon actually looked more like her mother than she normally did. Her eyes, clear and bright, danced around the black night as she talked on and on about her life back in Dallas. It sounded like a good life, a busy life that needed her to get back to it on time, by seven o'clock sharp on Sunday for the birthday party of her friend Sylvia. "I'm trying to convince Roland to move down to Dallas instead of me moving up here. I don't want to be far away from Mama and Daddy, they need me too much now. And I don't think I could live anyplace else but Dallas. It's in my blood. Dallas is just in my blood." She didn't seem as troubled about her future with Roland as she had in the past few days. "I know that I have loved a really decent, good man and no matter what happens, I know he helped heal me," she said looking up into the sky while she warmed her nose with her fingers.

Everyone loved the white artichoke lasagna. As for the cantaloupe and the green beans—eh—they sort of froze on the plates, but they looked *fab-u-lous-imo*. They were the perfect side dishes to a heavy meal. We picked off one another's plates as Evie's next-door neighbors poked their heads out their bedroom window to wave hello. We all laughed when they yelled to us, asking if we were all crazy or just plain nuts. Evie yelled back at them, "We're neither, we are a bunch of clever broads out here having ourselves a great time. You should come join us. It's fantastic out here." When Evie's smile caught the candlelight she looked like a breathtakingly stunning, pregnant woman. I ask you, is there anything more magnificent than a pregnant woman?

After Evie and Karen cleared away all of the dinner plates, Sharon brought out her banana cream goo cradled in a drippy pool of hot, buttery chocolate sauce, served in a champagne glass. "It's a butterscotch sauce, Junie. Don't say it was chocolate, that would sound awful." Whatever the hell it was, it had vanilla ice cream with spongy ladyfingers crammed in the center, floating in a puddle of butterscotch with sliced bananas on top. *It was hideous*, but everyone slurped it up, licking their spoons as they finished.

We stayed out on the terrace until our earlobes froze and we couldn't hear what the other one had said. I heard fragments of a story Sharon told about me that made Evie and Karen roll with laughter. "No, she did too . . . in college, Junie . . . and then she. . . . No, I swear to you she did it all of the time. . . . She was always that way . . . since the day I met her," she said, howling with laughter. No one would tell me what she said, they all just sort of smiled in my direction and nodded their heads. "You're right, Sharon . . . she really is, you are absolutely right. . . ."

I am what, damn it?

"The most neurotic person any of us has ever met —but it's what makes you so interesting."

———

Star light, Star bright,
Last star we see tonight.
We wish we may, we wish we might,
Be as happy as we are tonight.

May you know your dignity in this life.

Love always,
Junie, Sharon, Karen, Evie and baby girlie-girl
11:32 p.m.
December 6, 1993
New York, New York

White Artichoke Lasagna

3 tablespoons butter
½ cup plus 5 tablespoons
   olive oil
1 pound mushrooms,
   sliced
3 cloves garlic, minced
½ cup white wine
2 yellow onions, chopped
1 red bell pepper, seeded
   and diced
½ cup flour
3 cups milk
3 pounds ricotta cheese
8 ounces Parmesan
   cheese, grated

½ cup chopped parsley
Salt and pepper to taste
3 10-ounce packages fro-
   zen chopped spinach,
   thawed and drained
   thoroughly
2 pounds fresh asparagus
1 pound lasagna noodles
1 14-ounce jar marinated
   artichoke hearts,
   drained and
   quartered
1 pound mozzarella
   cheese, sliced

Preheat the oven to 350 degrees. In a large frying skillet melt the butter, and add 3 tablespoons of the olive oil and mushrooms and garlic. Sauté until the garlic browns. Add the wine and continue to sauté for 3 or 4 minutes. Strain the juices from pan and reserve them. Return the pan to the stove and add the ½ cup of olive oil, the onions and red bell pepper and sauté until the pepper is tender. Sprinkle the flour into the pan, stirring constantly, until it has a thick gravy-like consistency. Add a touch more olive oil if the mixture is too dry. Whisk in the milk, slowly stirring in to allow the sauce to continue to thicken gradually. Add the strained juices. Remove from heat and allow to cool.

    In a large mixing bowl combine the ricotta cheese, Parmesan cheese, parsley, salt and pepper, and the spinach, thoroughly drained of all water. (Don't precook it.) Set aside.

Trim the asparagus, reserving the tips only, 3 to 4 inches in length. Fill a large pot with 3 quarts water and bring to a boil, add asparagus tips and boil until tender crisp, about 3 minutes. Drain and refill the pot with 4 quarts of water. Add 2 tablespoons of the olive oil and bring water to a boil. Add the lasagna noodles and cook until al dente, 8 to 10 minutes. Drain and allow to cool.

Grease a 16 × 11 × 3-inch roasting pan with olive oil. Put a layer of cooked lasagna noodles, slightly over-lapping, on the bottom of the pan. Next, evenly spread half of the ricotta-spinach mixture on top of the noodles. Then layer half of the sautéed mushrooms, half of the asparagus tips and artichoke hearts, then another layer of the ricotta-spinach mixture. Cover with a layer of moz-zarella slices and repeat process: a layer of noodles, a layer of ricotta-spinach mixture, a layer of vegetables, a layer of mozzarella, finishing with a top layer of noodles. Sprinkle the top liberally with Parmesan cheese and bake for 1 hour and 15 minutes. Allow to cool for 15 minutes before serving; it will firm up and be easier to cut.

Note: Lasagna may be assembled a day ahead of time and refrigerated. If you are baking straight from the refrigerator, bake for 1½ hours.

Evie's Traditional Lasagna with Mint

3 medium yellow onions,
  chopped
1 stalk celery, chopped
1 green bell pepper,
  seeded and diced
3 cloves garlic, minced
½ cup plus 2 tablespoons
  olive oil
1½ pounds lean ground
  beef
1 pound sweet Italian
  sausage, casings re-
  moved and crumbled
¾ cup red wine
1 teaspoon salt
1 tablespoon red pepper
  flakes

2 28-ounce cans tomato
  puree
2 8-ounce cans tomato
  paste
1 teaspoon dried oregano
1 teaspoon dried mint
1¼ pounds lasagna
  noodles
3 pounds ricotta cheese
8 ounces Romano cheese,
  grated
3 tablespoons chopped
  parsley
Salt and pepper to taste
1½ pounds mozzarella
  cheese, sliced

Preheat the oven to 350 degrees. In a 4-inch deep skillet or soup pot sauté the onions, celery, green bell pepper and garlic in the ½ cup of olive oil until the vegetables are tender. Add the ground beef and sweet sausage and brown. Add the wine, salt, red pepper flakes and simmer for 10 minutes. Add the tomato puree, tomato paste, oregano and mint. Blend well and continue to simmer for 30 to 40 minutes.

While the sauce is cooking make the ricotta filling. In a large mixing bowl combine the ricotta cheese, Romano cheese, parsley and salt and pepper to taste. Blend completely and set aside.

Pour 4 quarts of water with salt and 2 tablespoons olive oil into a large pot and bring to a boil. Add lasagna noodles and cook until al dente, 8 to 10 minutes. Drain and allow to cool.

Grease a 16 × 11 × 3-inch roasting pan with olive oil. Spoon a layer of the sauce on the bottom of the pan, then add a layer of noodles, slightly overlapping, on top of the sauce. Next, spread a layer of ricotta mixture evenly across the noodles, then a layer of mozzarella slices and top with a layer of the sauce. Repeat the process twice more: a layer of noodles, a layer of ricotta, a layer of mozzarella slices, a layer of sauce. Finish with a top layer of noodles, remaining mozzarella slices and red sauce to cover.

Cover the lasagna loosely with aluminum foil and cook 1 hour. Remove the foil and cook for another 15 minutes. Allow to cool for 15 minutes before serving; it will firm up and be easier to cut.

Sautéed Green Beans with Lemon

SERVES 3 TO 4

1 pound fresh green
  beans
4 tablespoons butter
4 tablespoons chopped
  chives or scallions
2 tablespoons chopped
  fresh dill or thyme

2 teaspoons fresh lemon
  juice
1 teaspoon lemon zest
Salt and pepper to taste

Trim the green beans and cut into pieces. Add to a sauce-pan of boiling, salted water and cook until tender-crisp. Remove from heat, drain and set aside.

In a large skillet melt the butter. Add the chives or scallions, dill or thyme, lemon juice and zest. Add the cooked beans and sauté gently until warmed. Add salt and pepper to taste.

Sharon's Banana Cream Goo

SERVES 4

1 package of ladyfingers
2 ripe bananas, peeled
    and sliced
1 carton of vanilla ice
    cream

1 cup chocolate sauce (or
    butterscotch, if you
    must)

Mash an unsplit ladyfinger into the bottom of a red wine glass or goblet that could display this crap. Drop a few slices of banana into each glass and layer with ice cream, chocolate sauce and ladyfingers, and top with sliced bananas. Serve cold and deny you ever made anything this bad.

If you hate this recipe, call Sharon. I don't want to know about it.

Where the Rubber Meets the Road

*F*or better or for worse Bucky and I remain together.

My panic attacks returned moments after our reunion at the Lemon Tree Motor Lodge. The flight to Atlanta was delayed due to fog, and I arrived late to the brown stucco roadside motel. Bucky was frightened I'd changed my mind. When I saw him standing in the doorway of room 8-H he was a little remote as he leaned down to give me a thin-lipped kiss. He was barefoot, wearing blue jeans and no shirt, drinking a warm Heineken straight from the bottle. "We missed dinner with some of my buddies. I wanted them to meet you."

I leaned against the doorway and stared at him until he took my bag from my hand. We said nothing as he set it near the closet and seated himself at the foot of the bed. "Do you want to come in and stay, Junie?" I walked over to Bucky and kissed him for what felt like an extremely long time. His skin was still warm and moist from the shower and I could taste the faint essence of Heineken in my mouth. I didn't scratch once as Bucky pulled different layers of clothing off of me and I lay naked on top of a kelp green polyester bedspread. It was just getting dark outside. Bucky moved his hand very slowly over my right breast as I stared at an oil painting of a circus clown near the door, which was still open. "Don't leave me now, Junie. Please don't." And so I didn't. We made love very slowly and quietly until we heard people talking in the hallway. Bucky lifted himself off me to close the door as I crawled into white polyester sheets and fell asleep. When I awoke his hand was holding mine as he slept beside me. I couldn't breathe any air into my lungs; somewhere in my sleep a suffocating terror had set in. The back of my neck was soaking wet and I was trembling in a cold gasping sweat. I felt that way I used to always feel, like I was dying. I pulled my clammy hand slowly from his grasp and rolled up on my side like an overgrown fetus and trembled until I felt Bucky's hand rub my back. He held me for hours as I sobbed into my pillow. It is so hard for a loner like me to let love in after so much time alone. In his quiet way Bucky understood this and said nothing as he stroked my hair. I don't know which is harder—to learn to comfort yourself or to allow someone to comfort you in a way that makes you a part of them.

Before we went to bed that night Bucky and I split a Baby Ruth and a Butterfinger from the vending machine in the lobby. We said very little to each other before drifting off for a final sleep. He held on to my hand all night and I got used to it after a while. Bucky went to the racetrack early the next morning while I stayed in bed watching the Home Shopping Club. I called Karen to tell her that Tova Borgnine's skin care line looked like an investment we should share in together. She asked me if I loved Bucky and I told her I was grateful for him. As if God had sent me someone to heal those places in my heart that I could not get to on my own. We cried together as she opened a box of Frosted Flakes for dinner. "We don't do things like that anymore, remember, honey? You've got to fix yourself something to eat and take care of yourself," I said, laughing with tears in my eyes.

During the conversation I made the innocent mistake of telling Karen that Bucky had a very large, slender penis. Karen in turn innocently told Evie about Bucky's penis later that day during a brief conversation regarding the baby's room. Evie then blurted it out to Sharon while on the phone to her in Dallas. Later, Sharon called me in hysterics, telling me to keep my trashy mouth shut about the size and shape of her baby brother's penis. Bucky got wind of this when he returned from the track that evening while I was still on the telephone with her. "Jesus, Junie, couldn't you have just said it was extremely large and left it at that?" I smiled up at him as he shook his head. "Well, at least it got you to smile," he said as he winked at me.

Later that night Bucky and I went to Ryan's Family Steakhouse and ate hot beef sandwiches with lots of mashed potatoes and gravy. Over dinner he made me promise to come to the racetrack with him in the morning to meet his buddies, which I cheerfully agreed to do. We didn't make love that night since Bucky fell asleep while I was giving him a back rub. He liked it when I poured tiny drops of lavender oil down his spine and massaged it deep into his muscles. I spent most of the night waking him up with little kisses. "Come on, Junie, let's get some sleep now," he said, petting my head. Sometime before sunrise Bucky woke me up and we made love. Afterwards he asked me if I was going to be all right. I smiled at him and he kissed the tips of my fingers. He seemed a little concerned.

I average about three races a month and have seen parts of this country I never knew existed. (I have also seen a wide variety of dopey sluts who canvas the parking lots of these racetracks with their breasts hanging out of their bathing-suit tops. It's wall-to-wall dopey sluts parading around waving to Bucky and his racing buddies from behind the wire fence. Bucky seems irritatingly familiar with many of them. One of the drivers' wives, who is a nurse, explained that it's part of the business of stock car racing—migrating caravans of dopey sluts. *Does every woman in the South have big, friendly breasts?* The wives and girlfriends of Bucky's buddies all seem very level-headed about the racing groupies. Where as I, on the other hand, tend to glare at them a lot.)

Although most of my weekends are spent with Bucky, I still live as a single woman in New York. Most weeknights I have dinner with Karen or go over to Evie's and hang out on the terrace with her and Sol. Evie had a beautiful baby boy, who they named Carl after her father who died when she was a teenager. Sol cooks and cleans and takes care of the baby now that Evie has returned to work full time. In the beginning, she was very anxious about leaving the baby, but now I think she feels a little better about it. Sol bought a vegetable juicer and is driving everybody nuts with his carrot and spinach juice cocktails. They taste worse than shit. "He says he'll never touch another vodka martini as long as he lives. He's starting to remind me of Richard Simmons. We're gonna have to have a talk about this." But nothing makes

Evie happier than when she sees Carl's sunny little face staring up at her in the morning before she goes to work. On the weekends she puts him in his plastic car seat and sets him on the kitchen counter. "Carl and I cook together now. I'm teaching him how to make goulash." I don't think Evie ever thought her life would turn out to be this stable and secure.

People magazine did a brief article on "Aging Super-Model Turned Artist." The picture of Karen that ran with the story was unlike any reflection ever taken of her. A few pounds heavier than she would like to be, she was seated on the floor in a sea of colorful chips of tile and semi-precious stones. There was no trace of makeup or jazzy earrings to confuse her image—just her face bathed in light, relieved from any pretense or worry. She got a lot of response from the story and is currently working on a tile mosaic for some lady's pool in Rumson, New Jersey. I'm going to go out and help her get set up and run any odd errands. She has not dated since she broke up with Steve and seems very content to remain alone until she meets someone different from who she has picked in the past. Her favorite thing to cook these days is homemade granola made with cashews, sunflower seeds, raisins and dates. I'll include the recipe.

I am going to see Sharon next weekend when I meet Bucky in Dallas to celebrate Daddy Snorkel's seventieth birthday. Mama is planning a small barbecue and I promised to make potato salad. Daddy Snorkel put us both on notice to be on our best behavior because Mama Snorkel has suffered a major tragedy in her life. Her beloved apricot-glazed toy poodle, Eclair, accidentally drowned while sipping water out of Daddy Snork's toilet. It seems as if Eclair must have slipped somehow and wound up banging his furry skull against the bottom of the bowl. Luckily, Daddy found her and spared Mama the trauma of seeing

Eclair bottoms up. Bucky bought her a Chihuahua and will be surprising her with it when we serve Daddy's birthday cake. I told Bucky of Eclair's ugly demise while we drove to the Charlotte airport. We looked at each other and burst out laughing until there were tears running down our cheeks. "What a way to go, man . . . in a toilet bowl," he said, rubbing his eyes. Now every time either of us mentions Eclair's name, we start laughing.

Sharon failed to see the humor when Bucky tried to include her in our morbid amusement. According to Bucky, she wants to start her own business as a party planner. I am sure Daddy Snork will be bankrolling her latest venture, which will cause problems with Roland. He doesn't understand why she won't move to New York and be his live-in girlfriend. Sharon flatly refuses, saying she wants her own earth beneath her feet. My sense is that she needs to find a man earthed from the same spiritual pod as she, someone who will recognize her deep need for communion with the man she loves. Roland doesn't seek that deeply within himself to find that place where two spirits meet, so it keeps her praying for more insight and courage to find what she is looking for—a man with a generous spirit. Mama agrees with me.

As for Bucky and me there are still many nights that I awaken gasping for air in a cold dripping sweat. I will not deceive you, it has been very hard on us. He seeks so desperately to quiet my suffering and I never seem to stop asking for his forgiveness. Those moments always bring us closer after they have passed because, like myself, Bucky too is by nature a loner. It relieves him that I don't pressure him into marrying me. I don't think either of us is a reliable candidate for marriage. We feed each other in a way that makes us capable of living alone, yet not disconnected from experiencing love. He roots me in a way that makes me not fear life so much. In return, I love him in a way that doesn't make him feel like his wings are clipped. He is free to roam the earth and know he is loved—deeply, deeply loved. It's not a relationship that would satisfy most people, but for us it quiets a need to wander alone in the world and not have it feel like a Godless existence. In the meantime, while I continue to feed myself, I am learning to also feed another.

It takes practice.

Karen's Quick Granola

*4 cups health-food store
granola (from one of
those bins)*
1 cup bran cereal
*½ cup raw sunflower
seeds*
*¼ cup cashews, raw or
toasted*
½ cup raisins

½ cup dried dates, pitted
½ cup coconut flakes
*½ cup dried banana
chips*
*2 teaspoons ground
cinnamon*
*2 teaspoons ground
nutmeg*

Combine all the ingredients in a large mixing bowl. Store
in an airtight container.

Acknowledgments

With my hands shaking and tears running down my face I will try to thank all of my friends, who gave me faith that someday, if I worked hard enough, I would get to be a writer. The names about to be mentioned are not listed in matters of importance, rather from memory, which at the moment is very clouded with emotion.

Thank you, E. Jean Carroll, for your loyalty and friendship. This book would have never been written had you not been there yelling at me to get off my fat ass and go write something. It's an honor to be your friend.

My deepest thanks to Geraldo and C.C. Rivera for sticking by me through all of those lonely, difficult days. I thank you both separately for encouraging me to write and for giving me the opportunity to be a columnist for the *Two Rivers Times*. You are both dear and wonderful friends.

Thank you, thank you, thank you to my editor, Christopher Schelling, who told me to write a novel. You, Christopher, inspired me, listened to me and always let me know that I was in good hands. Your confidence in me gave me courage, Christopher, tremendous courage.

To Carole DeSanti, I thank you for all your help and insight with this book. Thank you, Laura Ross, for all of your hard work and encouragement.

A thousand thanks to my friend and the best damn lawyer in New York City, Larry Shire. You've always taken good care of me, Larry, and I so appreciate it.

Thank you Mary Lalli, for painstakingly testing all of my recipes and for making sure they all tasted exactly right. I threw you a thousands slips of culinary confusion and iffy measurements and you made sense of it all. Please write a cookbook, Mary, the world needs to see your talent.

Now to each and every one of my friends who I am forced to lump together due to lack of space; I will send all a private thank you. Renee Props: Our friendship is eternal. No one is more beautiful to me than you. Melody Anderson: Thank you for showing me what it means to be a woman with grace and backbone. Carol Perkins: You and I have done it all and are still around to see where we have come from. You are a remarkable person. Edie Yoeli: I'm sure you see your spirit in this book. You more than anyone inspired me to show the world what a great woman sounds like. Claudia Albetta: You taught me how to be a friend, and taught me how to show up for life. You taught me how to get some dignity into my life—I would have never made it without you. Christine Schommer: You are a blessing in my life, an incredible blessing. Anne Sexton: Junie and I both thank you for making sure the world never knows how illiterate we really are. You've been a true friend to me. Alana García: You're the best, honey. We gotta do another road trip to Maine—only this time with a map. Susan Kinsolving: You are truly, truly, truly one of the most talented writers I have ever met and a wonderful friend. I swear I am coming up to see you, William and the girls very soon! Collin Summers: I am living proof that a person can believe in God and learn to work a computer. Thank you for all those 2 a.m. phone calls. To my *wonderful Bobby Zarem!!!* I'm still waiting for my red sports bag, Bobby, that everyone but me got in Buffalo! I love you so much, Bobby!

To all of the friends who put up with me while I wrote this thing—Linda Stowlow, Vera Kock, Corynne Corbett, Myra Scheer, Wendy Sarashon, Susan Gray Smith, Robert Arseneau, Daryll Brown, Dennis Gilby, Betty Jane Hilton and Bruce Beirman: Thank you so much for understanding my constant pissing and moaning.

To my ministers, the Reverend Larry Amaar and the Reverend Paulo Santos, and the Johrei Fellowship: You showed me that God heals all suffering. From the deepest place in my heart, I thank you.

To Tom Cole and Jerry Lubenow: Thank you for your support and understanding.

To Matthew Bialer, my agent and friend: Thank you, thank you! William Morris is the lucky one.

To my sisters, Emily Huss Tashman and Ellen Huss, I love you both and appreciate all you have done to help me over the years.

Index

◎

RECIPES INDICATED BY BOLDFACE TYPE.